Critical Thinking Growth for Problem Solving and Decision Making

Create a Positive Mind Set for Thinking

Eric J Kelly

Table of Contents

Introduction:

Kindle the Fire—Your Journey to Critical Thinking Mastery

In 2010, the world witnessed a stunning example of what collective creative thinking can achieve when 33 miners were rescued from the depths of the San José mine in Chile (Pallardy, 2024). The mine, located in the Atacama Desert, collapsed on August 5, trapping the men 2,300 feet below ground. The mine's history of safety violations and outdated maps complicated the rescue, but perseverance and innovation prevailed.

For 17 harrowing days, the miners survived on minimal rations and water from a spring and radiators in sweltering heat and humidity. Their plight seemed hopeless until, on August 22, a drill probe brought back a note: *"All 33 of us are all right in the shelter."* This message sparked an unprecedented global effort.

Experts from diverse fields, including NASA scientists and mental health professionals, joined Chilean authorities to sustain the men and devise a rescue plan. Food, medical supplies, and communication tools were delivered through narrow drill holes as three massive drilling rigs—American and Canadian-operated—worked tirelessly to carve a path to safety.

On October 9, after weeks of grueling labor, the Plan B drill broke through. A specially designed metal capsule was then prepared for the rescue. In the early hours of October 13, after 69 days underground, the first miner was brought to the surface. By nightfall, all 33 were reunited with their families as the world celebrated a story of survival, ingenuity, and unity.

The rescue, meticulously coordinated and broadcast globally, showcased the power of human collaboration and resilience, leaving an enduring legacy of hope and determination.

"But what does the story above have to do with critical thinking?" you may well ask. Everything, as it would turn out.

Without the quick and often chaotic thinking of the people who led the rescue operation, the men could have remained stuck in the mine until December!

In today's fast-paced world, where complex decisions and constant challenges define daily life, the ability to think critically is more important than ever. Critical thinking is not just an academic skill; it is a life skill that underpins effective problem solving, sound decision making, and a positive, resilient mindset.

In modern society, critical thinking is no longer optional—it's essential. It empowers you to:

- discern real information from fake news.

- break down complex inputs into manageable parts.

- identify and overcome bias.

- embrace perspective shifts as opportunities for growth.

- make logical, informed decisions with confidence.

- reflect on your motivations and emotions to act with clarity and purpose.

Now, critical thinking isn't just about solving problems; it's evolved; it's about enhancing your mental health and overall well-being as well. A sharpened critical thinking skillset allows you to regulate emotions, manage stress, grow intellectually, and build the resilience needed to thrive in an unpredictable world.

If you've ever asked yourself, *"Can I demonstrate a rational point of view? Do I have the skills and mindset to navigate life's challenges thoughtfully?"* then this book is for you.

Still Undecided? Let's Take a Deeper Look!

Critical Thinking Growth for Problem Solving and Decision Making has been crafted to meet the needs of individuals like you who want to enhance their ability to think on different levels, break down challenges into manageable parts, and make informed decisions. In a world where mental health and well-being are deeply intertwined with how we perceive and process problems, developing critical thinking is not just a cognitive exercise—it's a pathway to a healthier, more empowered life.

Whether you're at a mental intersection, rekindling the fire within to turn toward a new direction, or simply seeking to bolster your cognitive abilities, this book is your guide to clarity, resilience, and growth.

This book is designed for adults at various stages of their thinking journey. You may be here because you want to:

- improve your mental health and well-being.

- develop a positive, resilient mindset.

- master thinking techniques to navigate life's curveballs with confidence.

- learn to make better decisions, and manage stress.

- frame the unexpected in a positive light.

No matter your reason for picking up this book, take pride in that your decision is a wise investment in yourself.

How This Book Works

To guide you effectively, the book follows a structured and ascending approach, utilizing the frameworks of Bloom's Revised Taxonomy (*Bloom's Revised Taxonomy*, 2019) and Marzano and Kendall's Taxonomy (Balino, 2023). You'll progress through six levels of thinking:

1. Remembering
2. Understanding

3. Applying

4. Analyzing

5. Evaluating

6. Creating

On the way, you'll also explore the *metacognitive system*, which, put simply, is how we think about our thinking and the *self-system* or how one's beliefs, emotions, and motivations influence their thinking.

You'll begin by building a solid foundation, developing skills one at a time, before combining them into a cohesive problem-solving toolkit. Each chapter is designed to grow your abilities step by step, ensuring you feel confident and capable as you progress.

With each chapter, you'll:

- build a positive mindset to tackle problems logically and creatively.

- gain the tools to disaggregate challenges, synthesize solutions, and make decisions with confidence.

- learn strategies to embrace change and frame the unexpected as opportunities.

- develop lifelong cognitive skills for personal and professional growth.

What You'll Learn

Whether you see this book as a personal positioning strategy, a gem of stoic literature, or an advanced thinking compass, the result is the same—you'll gain practical skills to navigate the world more effectively, from decision making to stress management, from intellectual growth to reflective self-understanding.

Reading this book will give you:

- a clear understanding of critical thinking and its impact on your life.

- techniques to disaggregate complex challenges into manageable parts.

- tools to pause, pivot, and strategize effectively, no matter how complex the situation.

- insights into how a positive mindset fosters better decision making and mental well-being.

- practical exercises to apply these skills in real-world scenarios.

Why This Book?

This book exists because critical thinking is evolutionary. It's a skill that can take you from surviving to thriving, helping you step forward at life's crossroads, whether to change and pursue a new direction or find the motivation to push ahead with positive self-belief.

Through this journey, you'll uncover the tools and mindset needed to adapt, innovate, and rise above challenges. You'll learn to see every problem as an opportunity to pause, reflect, and strategize effectively, and you'll be equipped to act with confidence and purpose.

As someone deeply invested in the science and practice of critical thinking, I've seen how transformative these skills can be. I've designed this book not only to share knowledge but to act as your guide on a learning journey that prioritizes clarity, growth, and empowerment. You can find my author bio and why I am uniquely qualified to write on all these subjects at the end of this book.

You're in the Right Place!

By picking up *Critical Thinking Growth for Problem Solving and Decision Making*, you've made a meaningful investment in your self-development. You will not only enhance your thinking skills but also cultivate a mindset that's resilient, adaptable, and prepared for life's uncertainties.

You've already made the first step by choosing this book. Whatever brought you here, you've decided to invest in yourself and your future. Together, we'll build the critical thinking skills you need to navigate life with a clear mind, a positive outlook, and the ability to turn challenges into opportunities.

Are you ready to develop your critical thinking and embrace a positive mindset that will elevate your decision making and problem-solving skills? If "yes," let's begin this journey together!

Test Your Thinking Level

You will be provided 6 statements from the Chile Mine Rescue. By choosing the statement that most closely correlates to your thinking you will gain an indication of your level. From there, this book will provide you with an incremental approach to advance your critical thinking.

https://880e-admin.systeme.io/criticalthinkinglevel

Section 1:

Higher-Order Thinking—Critical Thinking (CT)

Chapter 1:

Positive Critical Thinking and Mindfulness— The Power of Belief

Critical Thinking is the tool that helps individuals find answers or solutions to confusion and problems. –Plato (as cited in Changwong, Sukkamart & Sisan, 2018)

Anna, a manager at a tech company, is staring at her screen, overwhelmed by a cascade of emails, spreadsheets, and meeting notes. Her team's project—one she had passionately spearheaded—had hit a wall. Conflicting data, mixed stakeholder opinions, and an unforgiving deadline loomed over her like dark clouds.

Anna felt paralyzed. Should she stick to the original plan, knowing it could fail, or change it and risk alienating key players? Every decision seemed like a minefield. Deep down, Anna knew she had faced challenges before and come out stronger. Yet, this time, she needed more than gut instincts—she needed clarity and a way to cut through the noise.

If you've ever felt like Anna, you know that sinking feeling of being trapped in indecision. In such moments, critical thinking becomes your lifeline—a tool to convert overwhelming complexity into manageable steps.

Critical Thinking, Mindfulness, and Positive Psychology

Let's pause and consider this: critical thinking isn't just about being "smart" or having all the answers. It's about knowing *how* to think, not just *what* to think. You can think of it as a Swiss Army knife for your mind—a combination of tools like analysis, reasoning, evaluation, and several more; you can pull out whenever life throws you a curveball.

Peter A. Facione, a world-renowned author known for his work on measuring and qualifying critical thinking, puts together certain qualities that experts agree most good critical thinkers have (Facione, 1990). These include being:

- habitually inquisitive and focused on inquiry.

- well-informed and diligent about seeking relevant and accurate information.

- accepting of reason.

- open-minded, flexible, and willing to reconsider.

- fair in evaluation.

- cautious in decision making and judgment.

- reasonable in the selection of criteria.

- honest about personal biases.

- clear about issues.

- orderly in complex matters.

- persistent in aiming for results as precise as the subject and circumstances will allow.

Now, it is not enough that a person merely possesses the above traits; they must use them regularly to be considered a good critical thinker. Fortunately, no one is born a critical thinker. Or, putting it in a better way, all of us are born with the potential to be good critical thinkers. Critical thinking is not a magic switch you flip on but a set of skills you practice and develop, one step at a time.

Critical thinking includes:

- **Breaking the problem down:** Can you take a tangled problem and unravel it into smaller, solvable pieces?

- **Seeing the bigger picture:** Can you step back and see how the pieces fit together to make a unique whole?

- **Challenging assumptions:** Are you brave enough to question what you've always believed or practiced?

- **Making connections:** Can you find creative solutions by linking ideas in new ways and creating new patterns?

- **Self-reflection:** Do you take the time to ask yourself whether a course of action is the only or the best way forward?

In more academic language, one could define critical thinking as including (Facione, 1990):

- **Interpretation:** understanding and being able to express the meaning of different types of experiences, events, situations, conventions, beliefs, criteria, rules, data, procedures, or judgments. In real life, this might look like organizing and categorizing information, clarifying and understanding the significance of things around you.

- **Analysis:** identifying the relationship between an event, situation, or statement and its implications. We analyze things by examining ideas and identifying and analyzing arguments.

- **Evaluation:** assessing the credibility of facts, stated beliefs, opinions, experiences, situations, etc., based on logic and reason. One would determine the validity of claims and arguments to do this.

- **Inference:** attained by identifying and gathering the relevant information needed to draw a reasonable hypothesis, conjecture, or conclusion. In day-to-day life, a critical thinker would infer things by questioning evidence and considering alternatives.

- **Explanation of the conditions on which judgment is based:** stating and justifying a decision based on one's reasoning ability. It includes presenting valid arguments, justifying methods, and stating the final result.

- **Self-regulation:** constantly monitoring one's thinking processes and all the elements that contribute to it, with the aim of questioning, correcting, or bettering it. This could include self-examination of one's thoughts, beliefs, and opinions, as well as the correction of one's thinking mechanisms.

Now, if all this is too technical, you can think of each of the above elements as ingredients in a recipe. Individually, they're useful, of course, but when you combine them, they create something extraordinary. And here's the best part: just as with many other skills like cooking, driving, or swimming, the more you practice critical thinking, the more readily it will answer your call for help.

Critical Thinking is a Skillset, Not a Skill

One common mistake all of us make is in considering critical thinking as an ability. Critical thinking is often thought of in the singular. In reality, however, it is a combination of distinct skills such as:

- **Analytical thinking:** breaking down information into manageable components.

- **Creative thinking:** generating alternative ideas or perspectives.

- **Evaluation:** assessing the credibility and relevance of information.

- **Logical reasoning:** drawing logical conclusions from the facts available.

- **Metacognition:** monitoring and reflecting on your thinking process.

This combination is advantageous because no single skill can solve every problem. Instead, a multipronged approach adapts to the complexity of real-world challenges. For example, in Anna's case, we will see how she can use analysis to identify the problem, creativity to brainstorm potential solutions, and evaluation to weigh the pros and cons of each strategy.

But there's also a twist: Critical thinking works best when paired with **mindfulness** and a **positive outlook**. Let us look at these two elements.

Mindfulness

Mindfulness keeps you present and aware, helping you notice your thoughts and emotions without letting them take over. It is the flashlight that lets you see what's in your mental toolbox. It promotes an awareness of one's thoughts, emotions, and biases. It creates the mental clarity needed to assess situations objectively.

So, what exactly is mindfulness? Psychologists define mindfulness as being made of a "nonjudgmental moment-to-moment self-awareness" of what a person is involved in (Škobalj, 2018; Henriksen et al., 2020). In simpler terms, we can define mindfulness as focused attention on whatever one is doing without attaching any labels or prejudice to it. By the same logic, negative biases and automatic thinking or actions would be antonymous to mindfulness. Most experts agree that mindfulness helps regulate stress and improves the cognitive, emotional, and interpersonal functions of the brain. What is more, mindfulness can even help boost creativity (Henriksen et al., 2020).

Positive Thinking

Meanwhile, positive psychology, which focuses on strengths and fostering resilience, adds the emotional buoyancy to keep you motivated through challenges. It is the fuel that keeps you going. It focuses on what's *possible* instead of what's *wrong*, giving you the confidence to tackle challenges head-on.

Our brains are truly unique in that, from time to time, they undergo processes akin to both software and hardware upgrades in computers. Software upgrades for the brain would be the deeper complexity of thinking and feeling we experience as we mature. Hardware upgrades are the physical changes in the neurological pathways of the brain. The more a person is willing and adaptable to learning new things, their brain will forge new thinking routes and discard old ways of perception. Unlike what was believed a few years ago, our brains don't stop developing when we reach adulthood. With the right kind of mental exercises in place, we can continue to improve the efficiency of our brains, both in functioning as well as in structure throughout our lives. This ability of the brain to rewire itself is called neuroplasticity (Ackerman, 2018).

Critical thinking is amplified by a positive mindset, which, as we have just seen, can be inculcated. The ability to see silver linings, even in setbacks, keeps you open to learning and adapting. Research highlights that fostering optimism rewires the brain to handle stress and uncertainty more effectively (Laranjeira & Querido, 2022). Logically, this is why an optimist will always surpass a pessimist, no matter how skilled the latter might be. While an optimist can look at what needs to be done, a pessimist will always harp on what can't.

A positive mindset acts as a catalyst for critical thinking. When individuals are mired in negativity, their ability to think clearly and objectively diminishes. Positivity, on the other hand, broadens their perspective, enabling them to see possibilities where others see dead ends. The thing is, even the sharpest critical thinker can falter without a positive mindset. When you're stuck in a loop of negativity, your brain goes into survival mode, focusing on threats instead of possibilities. However, with positivity, your perspective shifts. You don't ignore setbacks but start seeing them as opportunities to learn. The more you practice looking for silver linings, the better you get at finding them—even in the darkest clouds.

So, how can you build this mindset? If you think there are shortcuts to rewiring your brain positively, alas, you are sadly mistaken. Positive and critical thinking starts with small steps. For instance, it could be writing down one thing you're grateful for every day. Positivity might be enhanced by celebrating your wins, no matter how tiny. Over time, such habits strengthen your mental resilience, making it easier to stay focused and confident when life gets tough. Even daily affirmations confirming your love and care for yourself can prime the brain toward resilience, enabling you to approach problems with attention and clarity rather than fear.

Together, critical thinking, mindfulness, and positive psychology form a triad of mental habits that empower you to face complexities like Anna's. They allow you to manage overwhelming situations by staying present, finding opportunities in setbacks, and making informed decisions without succumbing to emotional turbulence.

Critical Thinking in Practice: Transforming Overwhelm into Opportunity

Going back to Anna's situation, the steps for her to transition from overwhelmed to clarity involves first asking herself, "What's one thing I can do right now to bring clarity?"

The following are some answers she might need to address in her specific situation:

1. stakeholder needs

2. team challenges

3. the project's overall goal

This simple act of organizing information will give her a sense of control. Then, she can apply a critical thinking framework:

1. **Prioritize:** She can identify the top three issues that need immediate attention.

2. **Challenge assumptions:** Was the original plan truly the only way? There could be alternatives her team hasn't yet explored.

3. **Evaluate options:** Using a pros-and-cons list, she can weigh the risks and benefits of turning around the project.

In a step-wise manner, Anna slowly leans into a positive mindset. She reminds herself of her team's strengths and past successes, shifting her focus from fear to possibility. This mental reframing gives her the confidence to present a revised strategy—one that works.

So, what is the lesson from the above example? Clarity doesn't come all at once. It's about taking small, deliberate steps and believing each one will lead you closer to a solution.

A practical example of this may be when people make career switches. One career option might offer stability but feel uninspiring. The other path could seem exciting but be fraught with risks. People spend weeks agonizing over the decision, going in circles with "what ifs" and "maybes."

But if you can approach it systematically, you would list your values—creativity, and growth, or balance and security—and weigh each choice. Then, imagine your future self in both scenarios. Which choice feels more aligned with who you want to become?

The choice may still not be easy, but the above process is bound to bring more clarity for you to make your ultimate decision.

Now that we've explored the power of critical thinking, it's time to take things a step further. In the next chapter, we'll examine how to slowly transform your lower-order thinking skills into higher-order cognition.

Key Takeaways

- **Critical Thinking:** It's a toolkit of skills—analysis, reasoning, evaluation, and creativity—that help you approach problems systematically.

- **Mindfulness and positivity:** These practices enhance critical thinking by keeping you focused and resilient.

- **Practical steps:** Break problems into parts, challenge assumptions, evaluate pros and cons, and stay positive.

Action Steps

1. A recent problem I faced was _____. How could critical thinking have helped?

2. One challenge I am currently facing is _____. Can I break it into smaller parts and apply a critical thinking framework to tackle it?

3. Practice finding silver linings—List three positives in my life right now.

Chapter 2:

The Bigger Picture—Think Beyond the Facts

Men and women range themselves into three...orders of intelligence; you can tell the lowest class by their habit of always talking about persons; the next by the fact that their habit is always to converse about things; the highest by their preference for the discussion of ideas. –Henry T. Buckle

Alex, a high school student, finds history class tough because he relies on rote learning rather than comparison, contrasting, and analysis. For a test on World War II, while his teacher wanted the students to work on themes like leadership and strategies during the war, Alex chose to answer the questions based on memorized facts, such as dates and names, without exploring deeper connections. When the test included analytical questions like comparing the strategies of the Allies and Axis Powers or evaluating the impact of the Yalta Conference, Alex struggled, as rote memorization left him unable to construct answers that went deeper than mere facts. Scoring poorly, he felt frustrated and doubted his abilities. He was unable to understand why, despite mentioning so much accurate information in his answer sheet, he was unsuccessful in getting even an average grade.

Alex decides to enlist his teacher's help in understanding where he is falling short.

Why Move From Lower to Higher-Order Thinking?

Critical thinking is the engine behind transformative ideas, innovations, and movements that have reshaped society across eras and fields. It is the ability to question, analyze, and synthesize information in ways that transcend surface-level understanding, enabling individuals to tackle complex challenges and illuminate new paths. While the skill is often hard-won and honed through failure and perseverance, it remains indispensable for making impactful decisions, creating meaningful discussions, and fostering deeper connections with the world around us.

Polishing the Rough Stone: Learning Through Failure

Great thinkers and leaders have often faced failure before refining their critical thinking abilities and achieving greatness. Like a jeweler working with a raw gemstone, they persisted in polishing their perspectives and ideas until they shone with brilliance.

Take Steve Jobs, for example, whose initial ousting from Apple in 1985 was a turning point (Levy, 2025). Instead of succumbing to defeat, Jobs used the experience to reevaluate his approach to leadership and innovation. Founding NeXT and funding Pixar, he expanded his understanding of user experience and technology integration, lessons he later applied when returning to Apple. His critical thinking focused not just on creating products but also on reshaping how technology interacts with human lives. It led to groundbreaking innovations like the iPhone and iPad, revolutionizing multiple industries.

Similarly, Marie Curie, the pioneering scientist who discovered radium and polonium, faced numerous challenges, including financial hardships and skepticism from the scientific community owing to her gender (*Marie Curie the Scientist*, 2015). Yet her meticulous questioning and refusal to accept conventional wisdom allowed her to uncover the mysteries of radioactivity, paving the way for advancements in medicine and physics. Her story is a testament to the fact that failure and resistance are often the catalysts for deep, critical engagement with a subject.

There are innumerable others like Angela Davis, Iris Murdoch, Jeff Bezos, Jordan Peterson, Judith Butler, Martha Nussbaum, Ruth Chang, Sara Ahmed, Simon Sinek, Stephen Hawking, and Susanne Langer who have made their mark on the world with their critical thinking capabilities, despite the many challenges they faced.

So what has made these people persevere in their thinking? What made them stand out from the crowd? Let us see.

Deeper Connection With the Subject

At the heart of critical thinking is a deep connection with the subject at hand. Rather than skimming the surface, critical thinkers delve into the depths of an issue, exploring its intricacies and contradictions. This depth nurtures understanding, empathy, and innovation.

Angela Davis, a scholar and activist, exemplifies this principle in her lifelong engagement with social justice and equality (*Angela Davis*, 2010). Davis's work in examining systemic racism, prison abolition, and intersectionality demonstrates her ability to think critically about entrenched societal structures. Her deep connection to these issues has not only informed academic discourses but also inspired movements worldwide.

Similarly, in philosophy, Martha Nussbaum's critical exploration of emotions and ethics has revolutionized our understanding of human capabilities (Aviv, 2016). By connecting deeply with subjects like justice, compassion, and the role of literature in shaping moral reasoning, Nussbaum has demonstrated how critical thinking can bridge intellectual inquiry and practical human concerns, enriching both fields.

Igniting Discussions and Driving Innovation

Critical thinking thrives in discussion, where ideas are tested, refined, and expanded. It is not about arriving at a single "right" answer but about the process of exploration and collaboration.

Simon Sinek, well-known for his "Start with Why" movement, has sparked global conversations about leadership and purpose (*Simon Sinek at Amsterdam Business Forum 2025*, 2025). His emphasis on understanding the deeper motivations behind actions has transformed how organizations approach their goals. Through his critical examination of human behavior and business dynamics, Sinek has fostered dialogue encouraging leaders to think beyond mere numbers and profit and focus on creating meaningful impact.

Likewise, Judith Butler, a philosopher and gender theorist, has opened discussions about identity, gender performativity, and societal norms (Gleeson, 2021). By challenging traditional assumptions of gender roles assigned to men and women and engaging in nuanced debates, Butler has expanded our understanding of human identity and the structures that shape it. These discussions, though often contentious, have propelled cultural and academic progress, demonstrating the power of critical thinking in challenging the status quo.

The Process Over the Product

One of the most essential aspects of critical thinking is that it places a greater emphasis on the process of reaching an answer than on the answer itself. This approach fosters intellectual curiosity, adaptability, and creativity.

Stephen Hawking, for instance, spent decades grappling with the complexities of black holes, time, and the universe's origins (Editors of Encyclopedia Brittanica, 2025). His groundbreaking insights, such as Hawking radiation, emerged from a relentless process of questioning, hypothesizing, and revising. While his findings were revolutionary, it was his intellectual journey—marked by perseverance and adaptability in the face of his physical limitations—that truly defined his genius.

Philosopher Ruth Chang has explored what she calls the capabilities approach, where each one is encouraged to ask themselves and others, "What can an individual do or become?" (Chang, 2014) The idea is to consider developable abilities, opportunity, and freedom for each person. Her work relies heavily on the social, economic, and political opportunities that shape human existence. She insists that every person deserves a right to dignity and that governments should allow everyone equal access to health and well-being, safety and bodily integrity, imagination and intellectual growth, emotional fulfillment, rational decision making, social connections, nature, recreation and joy, autonomy and agency, and lastly, life itself. The aim of her discussions is not to reach a final idea but to play with ideas that can improve the quality of human existence.

A Skill for Everyone

While critical thinking may seem the domain of intellectuals and innovators, it is a skill that benefits everyone, from students to professionals across fields. Jeff Bezos applied critical thinking in building Amazon, beginning with how technology could revolutionize shopping

(*Jeffrey P. Bezos*, 2025). His ability to analyze market trends, predict consumer behavior, and take calculated risks transformed Amazon from a small online bookstore into a global e-commerce and technology powerhouse.

The philosopher and expert on original thinking, Caroline McHugh, has used critical thinking to analyze everyday experiences of the self in relation to how a person versus others perceive themselves. She makes a brilliant argument for developing and upholding your unique selfhood through interiority and finding authenticity in being yourself (McHugh, 2013).

Jordan Peterson, a clinical psychologist and author, encourages individuals to think critically about their lives through his work on personal responsibility and meaning (Howes, 2018). His emphasis on grappling with life's challenges rather than avoiding them resonates with many who seek to develop resilience and clarity.

Critical Thinking in Action: The Ripple Effect

The impact of critical thinking extends far beyond individual achievements. It has a ripple effect, inspiring others to think deeply, question assumptions, and contribute meaningfully to the world. Susanne Langer's work in philosophy and aesthetics expanded our understanding of art, symbols, and human expression, laying the groundwork for interdisciplinary studies in the arts and sciences (*Susanne K. Langer*, n.d.).

All of Iris Murdoch's novels and philosophical essays have explored the moral complexities of human relationships, challenging readers to confront their inherent and often unperceived biases and strive for greater empathy and self-awareness (Mason, 2021).

All the individuals we have mentioned above have one common quality. They have not only achieved personal success but have also contributed to societal progress, promoting a culture of inquiry and innovation. Whether sparking global discussions, driving innovation, or nurturing empathy, it is clear that critical thinking remains the most essential tool for shaping a better future—one question, one insight, and one connection at a time.

The Benefits of Critical Thinking: Unlocking Your Potential

Critical thinking is more than just a skill—it's a tool that can enhance every facet of your life. Whether you're solving problems, learning new concepts, or even reflecting on your own actions, cultivating this habit of thought offers numerous benefits.

First, critical thinking sharpens problem-solving skills. It encourages you to break down complex issues, evaluate solutions objectively, and make informed decisions. This structured approach leads to effective resolutions or will help you circumvent challenges more confidently.

In analyzing situations using a critical lens, creativity flourishes. Instead of sticking to conventional solutions, critical thinkers are more likely to explore unique approaches and generate innovative ideas. This synergy between analysis and imagination can open doors to fresh perspectives.

One of the greatest strengths of critical thinking lies in its transferability. It's a lifelong skill, benefiting not just academics but also professional and personal growth. The ability to assess information, weigh evidence, and make rational choices is invaluable in both the workplace and daily life.

In addition, this mindset makes learning easier and more enjoyable. You engage more deeply with material by understanding the "why" behind concepts rather than memorizing facts. This not only improves retention but also transforms learning into an exciting process of discovery.

Critical thinking also teaches you to organize and present information objectively. Whether writing reports or making arguments, you'll develop clarity and precision in communication, which is vital for conveying ideas effectively.

Finally, even self-evaluation becomes more accurate. By questioning your assumptions and reflecting on your decisions, you gain deeper insights into your strengths and areas for improvement. This habit fosters personal growth and builds resilience.

In a complex world, critical thinking empowers you to thrive by navigating information thoughtfully and embracing challenges with an open mind.

Critical Thinking in Practice: The Stages of Critical Thinking

Going back to Alex's example, he realizes that while he may need to memorize key historical dates, places, and names, he needs to ask questions. For instance, he has to figure out why the Allies used a specific operation to target the Axis forces occupying Northern Africa—probably linked to the unique terrain and other limitations there, while they used a completely different military tactic elsewhere. The more he started asking such questions, the easier it became for him to remember the details because it was no longer random episodes of history but a single story linked by multiple causes and effects.

Like Alex, we also need to upgrade our thinking mechanisms over time in order to make a mark in our chosen fields. Since critical thinking is a journey of self-awareness and growth, by understanding its stages, you can progress from passive thought to mastery, cultivating sharper reasoning and deeper insights. Here's a closer look at the six stages of critical thinking (*Critical Thinking in everyday life: 9 strategies*, 2017):

Stage 1: The unreflective thinker

At this stage, perhaps like Alex, we are unaware of the flaws and biases in our thinking. Decisions are often influenced by assumptions or emotions, and we fail to recognize the need for improvement. Growth begins with the realization that better thinking is possible.

Stage 2: The challenged thinker

Here, we start to notice problems in our thought processes. We recognize inconsistencies, biases, or gaps in our reasoning and begin questioning our conclusions. This awareness is the first step toward improvement, though it may feel uncomfortable.

Stage 3: The beginning thinker

Motivated by our newfound awareness, we attempt to improve our thinking. However, efforts are inconsistent and lack structure. While progress is made, without regular practice and strategies, growth remains limited.

Stage 4: The practicing thinker

At this stage, we commit to developing critical thinking as a habit. Recognizing that improvement requires effort, we apply strategies like questioning assumptions, analyzing evidence, and seeking diverse perspectives. Regular practice strengthens our skills.

Stage 5: The advanced thinker

With consistent practice, critical thinking becomes more refined. We approach problems with greater insight, use evidence effectively, and challenge our own beliefs constructively. This stage marks significant intellectual and emotional growth.

Stage 6: The master thinker

Here, skilled and insightful thinking becomes second nature. We navigate complex issues with ease, make sound decisions, and inspire others through our reasoning. Critical thinking is no longer an activity but a way of life.

As we advance from being an unreflective thinker to a master thinker, we will also learn how critical thinking comprises a diverse array of skills, each of which we can draw upon concurrently. We will explore more on this in the next chapter.

Key Takeaways

- **Failure and resilience:** These setbacks can help improve critical thinking skills because they allow you to think in new ways.

- **Deep-diving into subjects:** Critical thinking necessitates a look into the intricacies and contradictions of a subject. Conversely, looking at a subject more deeply sharpens critical thinking, too.

- **Debates and innovations:** Critical thinking enables discussions from all angles and drives innovations and disruptions in the status quo. It welcomes change.

- **The process is the most important part:** Thinking critically is not about arriving at the "right" answer but understanding how you can arrive at a solution logically and rationally.

- **Practical steps:** Identify the stage of thinking you generally fall back upon— unreflective, challenged, beginning, practicing, advanced, or master thinking.

Action Steps

1. **Unreflective thinker:** Can I recall a time when I made a decision based on assumptions or emotions rather than facts? How did it turn out, and did I realize the flaws in my thinking afterward?

2. **Challenged thinker:** Have I recently identified a bias or gap in my reasoning? How did becoming aware of this influence my approach to a problem or conversation?

3. **Beginning thinker:** When I try to improve my thinking, do I notice specific areas where I struggle (e.g., analyzing evidence, questioning assumptions)? What strategies have I attempted to address these challenges?

4. **Practicing thinker:** A situation where I deliberately applied critical thinking skills, such as evaluating multiple perspectives before making a decision, was _____. What regular habits can I implement to strengthen this approach?

5. **Advanced or master thinker:** A complex issue I resolved successfully by using insightful thinking was _____. How did my ability to question deeply, reason clearly, and remain open-minded contribute to the outcome?

Chapter 3:

The Bias Trap—Navigating Mental Shortcuts

The greatest enemy of knowledge is not ignorance, it is the illusion of knowledge. –
Daniel J. Boorstin

Leah, a researcher, was known for her enthusiasm but struggled with one flaw—her decision-making skills were based on instinct rather than deliberation. Uncharacteristically, for a scientist, she rarely questioned her assumptions or gathered sufficient information while making her personal decisions.

Leah was faced with a life-changing choice when the reporting manager at her company presented her with two options:

1. Accept a promotion that required relocating to another city, offering higher pay but little support or mentorship.

2. Stay in her current role, where she had a solid team and potential for gradual growth.

Leah felt overwhelmed. She couldn't decide and began asking friends, many not in her field, for advice. Most asked her to consider her long-term goals, evaluate her finances, and research the cost of living in the new city. Instead of taking their advice, Leah acted impulsively, accepting the promotion because it sounded glamorous and exciting and ignoring the doubts gnawing at her mind.

Within months, Leah was struggling in the new city. She underestimated the challenges of living alone, miscalculated her expenses, and felt isolated in her new role. When problems arose at work, her lack of a critical thinking framework meant she couldn't effectively analyze or solve them. Every issue, big or small, seemed monumental, and she began doubting her abilities.

Leah's is a classic case of how one often neglects to use the right tools for making a decision that could have lifelong implications.

Let us first explore why having a sound base in critical thinking is vital for nearly everything we do in life.

Why Should the Base be Strong?

Critical thinking is often touted as a fundamental skill for success in education, the workplace, and personal life. Yet, its very nature—abstract and nuanced—can make it difficult to define or measure. Many people talk about the importance of critical thinking, but few focus on what it entails or how to evaluate it effectively. This gap makes it crucial to identify measurable parameters that bring clarity to the concept. Critical thinking isn't just about knowing what to think; it's about mastering how to think, and several essentials can guide its evaluation.

Drawing Connections Between Ideas

One of the hallmarks of strong critical thinking is the ability to draw meaningful connections between seemingly unrelated ideas. For instance, consider someone analyzing climate change and its impact on economics. A critical thinker could identify how shifts in weather patterns influence agricultural production, which, in turn, affects global trade and food prices.

This skill is measurable through exercises that challenge individuals to link concepts across disciplines or contexts. For example, asking someone to explain how the principles of teamwork in sports might apply to workplace collaboration can reveal their ability to synthesize knowledge from varied areas.

When evaluating this skill, assess whether you can make clear, logical bridges between ideas, demonstrating depth in your thought process. On the contrary, a lack of connection or reliance on surface-level reasoning indicates room for growth in this area.

Appreciating Perspectives and Arguments

A critical thinker is adept at stepping into someone else's shoes and understanding the reasoning behind their perspective. This doesn't mean agreeing with every viewpoint but appreciating the subtleties that inform diverse opinions.

Consider a debate about the ethics of artificial intelligence. A strong critical thinker would weigh both sides: the potential benefits of AI in improving human lives and the ethical concerns about job displacement or data privacy.

Assessing this skill in yourself, you would need to articulate arguments for and against a position. Can you engage respectfully with opposing viewpoints and demonstrate a willingness to refine your stance when new evidence arises? Rigid or overly defensive responses often signal a lack of openness—a critical barrier to effective critical thinking.

Building Arguments Based on Reason and Logic

Critical thinking hinges on the ability to construct arguments grounded in solid reasoning. This involves using evidence, identifying premises, and drawing valid conclusions. The difference between a persuasive opinion and a reasoned argument is often subtle but vital.

Imagine asking someone why they prefer one public policy over another. A strong response would include evidence—statistics, case studies, or historical examples that bolster their reasoning. Conversely, vague or purely emotional justifications may indicate a weaker grasp of logical argumentation.

To evaluate this skill, focus on the structure of your reasoning—are your arguments coherent, well-supported, and logically sequenced? Encouraging practice with tools like debate exercises or structured essays can help you refine this essential skill.

Spotting Faults and Inconsistencies in Reasoning

A critical thinker doesn't just build arguments—they scrutinize them, too. The ability to identify logical fallacies, gaps in evidence, or inconsistencies is a cornerstone of effective thinking.

Take, for example, evaluating an advertisement campaign's success. A surface-level thinker might take increased sales as proof of the campaign's efficacy. A critical thinker, however, would probe further—could other factors, such as seasonal demand or competitor missteps, explain the uptick in sales?

To understand faults and biases in your thinking, present situations laden with flawed reasoning and ask yourself to dissect the argument. A keen eye for detail and a commitment to intellectual integrity ensures success here.

Systematic Problem Solving

Critical thinking thrives on a structured approach to problem solving. This means breaking complex issues into manageable components, evaluating potential solutions, and executing a plan of action.

For example, tasked with reducing a company's expenses, a critical thinker would identify key cost drivers, assess their impact, and prioritize actionable steps. They wouldn't leap to conclusions or fixate on minor details at the expense of the bigger picture.

Observe your approach during a multi-faceted problem. Do you employ a systematic method or tend to jump to conclusions? Remaining methodical under pressure is a clear marker of strong critical thinking.

Focusing on the "How" Over the "What"

Finally, the essence of critical thinking lies in asking how something works rather than passively accepting what is presented. This mindset fosters curiosity and a deeper understanding of underlying mechanisms.

For instance, instead of merely memorizing historical events, a critical thinker would explore how specific decisions led to outcomes, examining cause-and-effect relationships.

Try posing open-ended questions to yourself that require digging deeper into processes or causality. A lack of engagement with the "how" indicates superficial thinking, while thoughtful exploration reveals a critical thinker in action.

Critical thinking is not an abstract ideal but a practical necessity. As you refine the abilities above, you move closer to mastering the art of thinking not just clearly but critically—a skill that will empower you.

Laying the Foundation

Developing critical thinking requires a strong foundation built upon deliberate practices and frameworks. It is not an innate ability but a skill that thrives on mindful awareness, structured learning frameworks like Bloom's Taxonomy, and the integration of metacognition. These elements work together to enable people to think clearly, logically, and reflectively. Let us now explore these foundational pillars in more detail.

Mindfulness: Cultivating Awareness and Focus

Mindfulness is the cornerstone of critical thinking because it cultivates awareness, focus, and insight. Talking of critical thinking, mindfulness involves training your mind to observe situations calmly and objectively, enabling you to recognize biases, emotions, and assumptions that can cloud judgment.

For example, when faced with a challenging problem, practicing mindfulness can help calm reactive emotions, allowing you to focus on the issue systematically. A mindful thinker learns to pause, reflect, and approach problems with clarity rather than impulsivity. When you anchor yourself in the present moment, you can better engage with the logical processes required for critical analysis.

Practical mindfulness techniques—such as deep breathing exercises, journaling, or reflective meditation—can be integrated into daily routines to develop the calm, focused mindset essential for critical thinking.

Bloom's New Taxonomy: A Framework for Cognitive Development

Predominantly used in teaching-learning environments, Bloom's Taxonomy (*Bloom's Taxonomy*, n.d.) provides a structured approach to mastering critical thinking by guiding thinkers through six levels of cognitive complexity. It underscores the importance of progressing systematically, starting with foundational skills and moving toward higher-order thinking.

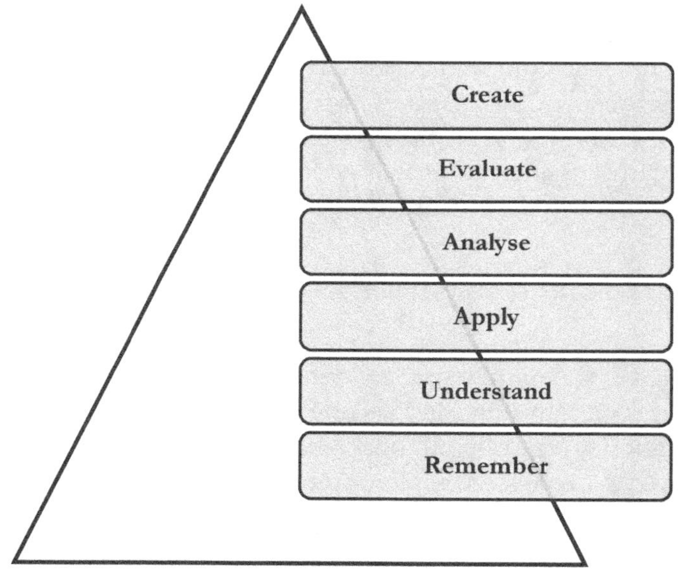

1. **Remember:** This foundational stage involves recalling facts, concepts, or procedures. Recalling key theories or definitions, for example, provides the knowledge base necessary for deeper analysis. Flashcards, quizzes, or summarization strengthen this level.

2. **Understand:** Understanding goes beyond memorization by requiring individuals to interpret or explain information. If you can rephrase a complex idea in your own words or explain it to someone, it fosters comprehension.

3. **Apply:** Application involves using knowledge in real-world contexts. One applies mathematical formulas to solve practical problems or historical lessons to analyze current events.

4. **Analyze:** At this stage, a person dissects information to identify patterns, relationships, and underlying structures. Analyzing a novel's themes or the arguments in a debate are examples of analytical thinking.

5. **Evaluate:** Evaluation requires making judgments based on criteria or evidence. This might involve critiquing a research paper, assessing the validity of an argument, or determining the feasibility of a proposed solution.

6. **Create:** The pinnacle of Bloom's Taxonomy is the ability to generate original ideas, solutions, or theories. For example, designing a marketing strategy, writing a persuasive essay, or proposing a scientific hypothesis reflects the creative synthesis of knowledge and critical thinking.

Practicing each level in sequence allows you to build the scaffolding necessary for advanced critical thinking.

Metacognition: Thinking About Thinking

Metacognition, which literally means "thinking about thinking," enhances the critical thinking process by fostering self-awareness and strategic planning. It involves understanding how you learn, setting goals, and evaluating your own progress. Marzano and Kendall (2007) have extended Bloom's Taxonomy to include a metacognitive system that interacts continuously with cognitive processes.

Setting Learning Goals

The metacognitive system begins by setting clear goals relative to new information. For instance, when tackling a complex subject, a metacognitive thinker might define specific objectives, such as mastering key concepts or understanding opposing viewpoints.

Designing Strategies

Once goals are established, metacognition involves designing strategies to achieve them. This might include breaking information into smaller parts, identifying areas of difficulty, or selecting appropriate tools and resources.

Continuous Interaction

Metacognition doesn't stop at planning—it involves ongoing interaction with cognitive processes. For example, while analyzing an argument, a metacognitive thinker might pause to assess their understanding or adjust their approach if they encounter challenges. This reflective loop ensures a deeper engagement with the material and encourages adaptability.

Metacognition, integrated into Bloom's Taxonomy, gives one the ability to monitor and regulate one's thinking, significantly enhancing their critical thinking capabilities.

In Practice

As we have seen above, even if the levels of critical thinking, as suggested by Bloom's Taxonomy, might be linear, the practice of critical thinking need not strictly be so. In other words, a good thinker knows, above all else, that ideas should never be set in stone and that they should be revisited in the light of new facts, information, or data.

Let's get back to Leah's case. How can she possibly get out of the situation she seems to have unwittingly landed in? At work, her turning point came when she confided in a mentor who asked her a simple question—"What criteria did you use to make this decision?" Leah froze, realizing she did not have one. The mentor suggested she revisit the foundations of decision making: defining goals, analyzing data, evaluating risks, and considering alternatives.

It wasn't easy, but Leah started building her critical thinking skills. She learned to pause, gather facts, and assess situations with a clearer mind. Slowly, she regained confidence and found ways to address her problems, turning daunting challenges into manageable tasks in her new workplace. In her personal life, she started being more methodical about income and expenses, taking the help of her colleagues in identifying and using cheaper alternatives where food, transport, and rent were concerned. Consciously making an effort to socialize with her new colleagues, she even made friends who supported her through the move, making her feel less lonely in the new city.

Leah's story reminds us that without a solid foundation for critical thinking, even the smallest problems can feel daunting, while thoughtful decision making can turn seemingly insurmountable issues into stepping stones for growth.

Key Takeaways

- **Drawing connections:** This helps connect the dots even between varied situations.

- **Appreciating different perspectives:** One can entertain different ideas even if one doesn't approve them all.

- **Building logical and rational arguments:** Reasoning and logic (and not emotions or assumptions) should be the bedrock of arguments.

- **Finding inconsistencies in reasoning:** Finding inconsistencies and gaps in reasoning will help improve critical thinking.

- **Systematic problem solving:** Critical thinking is a constant process of applying method and reason to problems.

- **"How" over "what":** Critical thinking gives precedence to the *how* of a problem rather than the *what* of it.

- **Bloom's Taxonomy:** This is a learning framework that lists the following strategies in increasing order of importance:

  - Remember

  - Understand

  - Apply

  - Analyze

  - Evaluate

  - Create

- **Metacognition:** Thinking about your thinking processes matters because one can set goals, revisit ideas, and improve strategies as required.

Action Steps

1. When faced with a challenging situation, how often do I pause to reflect before reacting? What can I do to cultivate greater calm and focus in these moments?

2. Which level of Bloom's Taxonomy do I tend to operate at most frequently (e.g., remembering, understanding, applying, analyzing, evaluating, or creating)? How can I challenge myself to engage with higher levels of cognitive complexity in my daily tasks?

3. Do I take time to set clear learning goals and evaluate my progress when tackling a new subject or problem? How could I improve my ability to monitor and adjust my thinking strategies?

4. In what ways has my critical thinking improved over time, and what specific steps or habits have contributed to that growth? What is one area of my critical thinking I'd like to strengthen further?

Chapter 4:

The Emotional-Logic Link—Bridging Emotional Intelligence and Critical Thinking

Watch your thoughts, they become words; watch your words, they become actions; watch your actions, they become habits; watch your habits, they become character; watch your character, for it becomes your destiny. —Frank Outlaw

Maya, a banking manager, is tasked with handling a conflict between two team members of the loans department, Alec and Priya. Alec accuses Priya of taking credit for his ideas during a client presentation. Priya counters that Alec's contribution was minimal and that her leadership brought the project to fruition. Both are visibly upset, and tensions are affecting the team's morale.

Maya feels torn. She values both employees and knows that resolving this conflict quickly is critical for the team's productivity. However, she struggles to balance her logical reasoning with the emotional dynamics at play. Maya feels overwhelmed by the conflicting perspectives. She's unsure whom to believe and worries about damaging her relationships with either Alec or Priya. Instead of addressing the issue head-on, she decides to send a vague email to both employees, encouraging them to "work it out among themselves." When tensions worsen, Maya grows increasingly frustrated with herself and her team. She begins to doubt her leadership skills.

Many of us have been where Maya stands. Her behavior—indecision, avoidance, and lack of engagement—stems from not fully integrating critical thinking and emotional intelligence into her approach.

Let us first look at what emotional intelligence is and how it contributes to critical thinking.

The Interplay Between Emotional Intelligence and Critical Thinking

In the quest for success, adaptability, and fulfillment, two prominent skills are critical thinking and emotional intelligence (EI). Though distinct in their focus— Critical thinking on the cognitive processes of reasoning and EI on understanding and managing emotions—the two are deeply intertwined. Together, they create a foundation for effective decision making, problem solving, and meaningful interpersonal interactions.

Critical thinking, as we have seen, is the ability to analyze, evaluate, and synthesize information in a logical, systematic way. It involves questioning assumptions, identifying biases, and applying reason to arrive at sound conclusions. It is primarily a cognitive process focused on objective analysis and the pursuit of truth or solutions.

EI, on the other hand, pertains to understanding and managing emotions—both one's own and those of others. It includes skills like empathy, emotional regulation, self-awareness, and effective communication. EI is rooted in feelings, centering on emotional awareness and interpersonal relationships.

While critical thinking and EI may seem unrelated at first—the first tied to thinking and the other to feeling—they are far from mutually exclusive. In fact, EI often strengthens critical thinking.

Empathy: A Key Bridge Between EI and Critical Thinking

Empathy, a cornerstone of EI, is indispensable in critical thinking, especially when dealing with human-centric challenges. Consider professions like teaching, medicine, or nursing, where understanding another person's perspective is crucial. In these fields, empathy enhances the ability to assess situations holistically, leading to better problem solving and decision making.

For example, a nurse faced with a patient's reluctance to follow treatment might use empathy to uncover emotional barriers—such as fear or mistrust—that a purely logical approach might overlook. A medical professional can achieve a more effective outcome by addressing a patient's emotions empathetically while applying critical thinking to devise a practical solution.

Empathy doesn't compromise logic; it enriches it by ensuring that solutions are both reasoned and compassionate. This is particularly important in resolving conflicts, mediating disputes, or making decisions that affect others.

Enhancing Learning Through the Fusion of Critical Thinking and EI

The integration of EI into the learning process significantly improves the quality and effectiveness of education. When learners develop EI, they become more adept at managing the frustrations, anxieties, or uncertainties that can hinder critical thinking.

For instance, a student who learns to regulate exam stress can approach problems with greater focus and clarity, enabling them to analyze and solve questions more effectively. Moreover, EI fosters a growth mindset, allowing individuals to view challenges as opportunities for improvement rather than insurmountable obstacles.

Incorporating empathy into learning also enhances collaborative efforts. Whether in group projects or workplace training, emotionally intelligent individuals are more likely to listen actively, respect differing perspectives, and contribute constructively—all of which are essential for developing critical thinking.

Managing Emotions: A Pillar of Resilient Thinking

Critical thinking often involves grappling with uncertainty, conflict, or emotionally charged situations. Without EI, a clouded judgment could easily fall prey to impulsive decisions.

Consider a manager mediating a workplace dispute. If the manager lacks emotional regulation, their own frustration or bias could exacerbate the conflict. However, an emotionally intelligent manager would remain calm, empathetic, and focused, allowing them to apply critical thinking effectively and resolve the issue constructively.

EI teaches individuals to recognize and manage their emotions, ensuring that feelings like anger, fear, or stress do not derail logical reasoning. This emotional control is essential for maintaining clarity, especially in high-pressure situations.

Benefits of EI

Developing EI brings a host of benefits, many of which directly complement and enhance critical thinking:

- **Improved self-awareness:** When you reflect on your thought processes and biases by understanding your emotions, strengths, and weaknesses, it fosters personal growth and sharper decision making.

- **Enhanced emotional regulation:** Managing stress and avoiding impulsive reactions allow you to maintain focus and reason under pressure, essential for critical thinking.

- **Better relationships:** Effective communication and empathy improve interactions, whether in romantic, familial, or professional contexts. These relationships create environments conducive to collaborative thinking and problem solving.

- **Higher resilience:** EI reduces burnout and improves coping mechanisms, helping you maintain critical thinking during stressful or adverse situations.

- **Stronger leadership and workplace performance:** Leaders with high EI excel in conflict resolution, team-building, and motivation, which are crucial for creating a positive and productive work environment. Emotionally intelligent leaders balance empathy with logic to make informed decisions that resonate with their teams.

- **Improved decision making:** EI encourages balanced responses to challenges, ensuring decisions are rational and thoughtful, even in emotionally charged scenarios.

- **Increased empathy:** By understanding and validating others' emotions, you build trust and deeper connections, facilitating cooperative problem solving.

- **Boosted well-being:** EI contributes to life satisfaction and confidence, enabling you to approach challenges with a positive and open mindset.

- **Enhanced adaptability:** EI equips you to navigate changes and challenges with resilience and optimism, which is essential for adapting critical thinking to new contexts.

- **Conflict management skills:** With EI, you can handle disagreements constructively, minimizing escalation and finding mutually beneficial solutions.

Critical thinking and EI are not opposing forces but complementary skills that, when combined, lead to exceptional outcomes. critical thinking ensures that decisions are logical and evidence-based, while EI ensures those decisions are empathetic and considerate of human factors.

For instance, a teacher deciding how to address a struggling student can use critical thinking to guide themselves to analyze the student's performance data and identify areas for improvement. EI, however, would let the teacher empathize with the student's struggles, communicate supportively, and create an action plan that takes into account the student's academic and emotional needs.

Even in leadership, a combination of critical thinking and EI allows leaders to make well-reasoned decisions while fostering trust and morale within their teams. A leader who listens empathetically and reasons logically is far more effective than one who relies solely on leveraging the skills of their team.

In Practice

In light of EI, let us look again at Maya's case. How can she manage the situation better in the future?

- **Applying EI: Understanding and managing emotions**
  - **Self-awareness**: Maya can recognize her feelings of discomfort and fear of conflict, allowing her to address them rather than letting them dictate her actions.
  - **Empathy**: Instead of treating the situation purely as a logical problem, Maya can take time to listen empathetically to both Alec and Priya, acknowledging their emotions and frustrations.
  - **Relationship management**: Fostering open communication and demonstrating fairness, Maya should strive to create a safe space for resolving the issue constructively.

- **Using Critical Thinking: Logical problem solving**
  - **Analyzing the situation**: Maya can gather facts by reviewing the presentation, seeking input from other team members, and evaluating Alec's and Priya's contributions objectively.
  - **Evaluating solutions**: She should consider potential solutions, such as mediating a discussion between Alec and Priya or implementing clearer guidelines for acknowledging contributions within team projects.
  - **Decision making**: Weighing the evidence and considering the team's dynamics, Maya can make a reasoned decision about how to move ahead.

- **Integrating EI and Critical Thinking**
  - To approach the situation with a balanced mindset, Maya can:
    - begin with an empathetic conversation to address emotions.
    - transition to a structured discussion focused on evidence and solutions.
    - use active listening and transparent reasoning to build trust while resolving the issue effectively.

In learning to integrate EI and critical thinking, Maya fosters a resolution that addresses both the emotional undercurrents and the practical concerns. All teammates will feel heard and respected, even if the final decision doesn't fully align with their individual perspectives. Team morale will improve, and Maya will feel more confident and effective as a leader.

Since interpersonal challenges are part of any human dynamic, personal or professional, the combined powers of EI and critical thinking are always going to be an asset in any given situation.

Key Takeaways

- **Critical Thinking and EI are distinct but interconnected skills:** Critical thinking focuses on logical reasoning and objective analysis, while EI centers on understanding and managing emotions. Logical reasoning ensures decisions are sound, while emotional awareness ensures they are compassionate, making this combination essential for personal and professional success. Together, they create a balanced approach to decision making and problem solving.

- **Empathy enriches Critical Thinking:** Empathy, a key component of EI, improves outcomes in human-centered contexts like teaching, medicine, and leadership. It helps bridge the gap between logical solutions and emotional needs.

- **Managing emotions is critical for effective decision making:** EI helps manage stress, regulate emotions, and maintain focus, enabling you to approach challenges with clarity and persistence.

- **Developing EI has wide-ranging benefits:** Improved self-awareness, better relationships, stronger leadership, enhanced adaptability, and increased resilience are just a few of the positive outcomes of building EI. Whether addressing conflicts, navigating challenges, or leading others, the integration of critical thinking and EI leads to more thoughtful, empathetic, and impactful actions.

1. When faced with a decision, do I take the time to consider both the logical aspects and the emotional impact on myself and others? How can I improve at balancing these perspectives?

2. How well do I manage my emotions, particularly in high-pressure or conflict situations? What strategies can I use to stay calm and focused to make better decisions?

3. In conversations or problem-solving scenarios, do I actively try to understand the feelings and perspectives of others? How can I use this understanding to create more effective and compassionate solutions?

4. How do I handle feedback, challenges, or mistakes? Do I approach them as opportunities for growth, and how can I use both critical thinking and EI to tackle them more effectively?

Chapter 5:

The Thinking Toolkit—10 Critical Supports for Smarter Decisions

Critical thinking is the disciplined art of ensuring that you use the best thinking you are capable of in any set of circumstances. –Richard W. Paul

Tim, a youngster, frequently relies on social media and online reviews to make purchasing decisions. Recently, he came across a glowing review for a "miracle" fitness supplement that promised rapid weight loss without diet or exercise. Excited by the bold claims, he immediately ordered a six-month supply, ignoring his friend's suggestion to research the product further. Tim trusted the review simply because it was written by a popular influencer, assuming their large following validated their expertise, despite no evidence of the influencer's qualifications. He focused only on the positive reviews that reinforced his desire for a quick fitness solution, ignoring negative reviews or critical discussions about the product. He assumed the supplement alone was responsible for the influencer's fit appearance, overlooking other factors like exercise, diet, or photo editing.

Do you see how easily the daily decisions we make could be manipulated by hype, faulty assumptions, and inadequate research? Well, we shall look at 10 remedies that might help us counter these logical fallacies in any situation.

The 10 Indispensable Cognitive Supports

I 5W2H Analysis

The 5W2H method is a structured approach to problem solving that focuses on seven key questions: **What, Why, When, Where, Who, How,** and **How Much**. This technique can break down complex problems into manageable components, ensuring all facets of a situation are considered systematically.

Benefits:

Clarity	Encourages clear identification of the problem and its context.
Comprehensive analysis	Covers all critical dimensions, reducing oversight.
Efficiency	Streamlines decision making by organizing information logically.
Flexibility	Adapts easily to various contexts, from business to personal challenges.
Enhanced collaboration	Provides a common framework that teams can use for effective communication and planning.

The 5W2H method can come to your aid in business strategy, project management, root cause analysis, and even personal goal-setting. For example, it can help define objectives (What), assign responsibilities (Who), set deadlines (When), and plan execution (How)

Some questions you can frame in the light of this method are:

- **What:** What are the desired outcomes? What resources are needed to address this issue?

- **Why:** Why is this issue occurring? Why is it important to solve this problem now?

- **Where:** Where is the issue most prevalent (e.g., department, location)? Where will the solution be implemented?

- **Who:** Who is affected by this problem? Who will address the issue?

- **How:** How can the solution be implemented? How can progress be monitored and measured?

- **How much:** How much time, money, or effort will this problem require in solving it? How much impact will the solution have on the organization or individual?

The 5W2H method helps individuals and teams approach problems with greater confidence, ensuring thoughtful and actionable solutions.

II SCQA Analysis

The SCQA method is extremely helpful in business communication, project management, and academic writing, with its clear emphasis on breaking down the issue into easily comprehensible components and stating a well-rounded solution.

The acronym stands for:

1. **Situation:** One can begin by establishing the context, outlining the background, and providing baseline knowledge. This sets the stage for understanding.

2. **Complication:** Next, introduce the problem, challenge, or conflict disrupting the situation. Highlight why it needs attention.

3. **Question:** Then, pose a clear and focused question addressing how to solve or mitigate the complication. This directs attention toward the core issue.

4. **Answer:** Finally, present a well-reasoned solution, including actionable next steps or recommendations to resolve the complication.

Benefits:

Clarity	Provides a clear and concise structure for presenting information.
Focus	Keeps the communication targeted on the problem and its resolution.
Persuasiveness	Engages the audience by highlighting complications and leading them logically to solutions.
Adaptability	Can be applied in various contexts, from professional to academic.
Action-oriented	Encourages practical and actionable outcomes.

SCQA enhances communication effectiveness by combining context, problem analysis, and solution-driven thinking.

III Top-Down vs. Bottom-Up Problem Solving

These two problem-solving methods are closely linked in their similarities and dissimilarities. We shall try to capture their main aspects via the table below:

Aspect	Top-Down Approach	Bottom-Up Approach
Definition	Starts with the overall goal or big picture and breaks it into smaller, manageable components.	Begins with specific details or tasks and builds toward a comprehensive solution.
Benefits	- Provides clear direction and structure. - Simplifies complex problems by segmenting them. - Ideal for projects requiring strong leadership and centralized control.	- Encourages innovation and different ideas. - Leverages detailed understanding from the ground level. - Adaptable to changing requirements or feedback.
Applications	- Strategic planning - Large-scale projects - Corporate policies and decision making - Software architecture	- Creative problem solving - Grassroots initiatives - Agile projects - Identifying solutions through experimentation
Ideal Scenarios	- When clear objectives are already defined. - For hierarchical organizations or highly structured projects.	- For exploratory projects requiring iterative development. - In dynamic environments needing adaptability.

Decision Making	Centralized: Decisions are made by higher-level management or leaders.	Decentralized: Decisions are driven by teams or individuals working on specific tasks.
Focus	Emphasizes the overarching framework or strategy.	Focuses on operational details and gradual refinement.
Limitations	-May overlook ground-level insights. - Risk of being rigid or disconnected from execution challenges.	- Can lack coherence without overarching direction. - Risk of inefficiency or misalignment with overall goals.

IV Logic Tree

A logic tree is a visual problem-solving tool that systematically breaks down a problem, goal, or decision into smaller, more manageable components. It starts with a clearly defined objective at the top and branches into categories and subcategories that provide deeper insights. It can be used in strategic planning, root cause analysis, process optimization, or project management.

Benefits:

A logic tree helps in:

- clarifying complex problems

- ensuring systematic and logical analysis

- encouraging mutually exclusive and collectively exhaustive (MECE) thinking for thoroughness

- facilitating data-driven decision making

Building a Logic Tree

1. **Define the objective:** Clearly state the main problem or goal at the top, ensuring it is specific and measurable.

2. **Segment the problem:** Divide the objective into mutually exclusive and collectively exhaustive (MECE) categories.

3. **Develop sub-branches:** Break down categories further into detailed factors or subcategories.

4. **Use a logical structure:** Maintain a hierarchical format, progressing from broad to specific concepts.

5. **Validate completeness:** Ensure all relevant factors are included, and the logic flows consistently.

6. **Analyze and test:** Use the tree to test assumptions or analyze data at each level, refining if needed.

7. **Present with clarity:** Make the tree visually clear and highlight key focus areas.

V Decision Tree

A decision tree is a graphical representation of decisions and their possible consequences, including probabilities, costs, and benefits. It uses a tree-like structure, where each branch represents a choice, chance event, or outcome, helping visualize the decision-making process.

This method is an excellent tool for business strategies, risk management, product development, medical and personal decisions, and so on.

Benefits

Clarity in decision making	Simplifies complex decisions by visually mapping out options and consequences.

Incorporates probabilities	Allows for the inclusion of uncertainty and likelihoods of outcomes.
Encourages comprehensive analysis	Breaks down decisions into smaller components, ensuring no factor is overlooked.
Flexibility	Easily adjustable as new data or scenarios emerge.
Supports quantitative analysis	Can calculate expected values to identify the most beneficial options.
Improves communication	Clearly communicates decision pathways to stakeholders or teams.

Creating a Decision Tree

1. **Define the decision:** Identify the decision to be made or the problem to solve. Write this decision or problem statement at the root of the tree. **Example:** "Should we expand our business to a new market?"

2. **Break down choices:** List all possible options or decisions as branches extending from the root. Ensure each branch represents a viable alternative. **Example choices:** "Expand to Market A," "Expand to Market B," "Delay Expansion."

3. **Consider consequences:** For each choice, branch out further with potential outcomes (positive and negative). Analyze implications such as costs, risks, or benefits. **Example outcomes** could be "Increased revenue," "High competition," "Unforeseen expenses," etc.

4. **Incorporate criteria for evaluation:** Add criteria like feasibility, alignment with goals, or ethical considerations to each branch. Use these to gauge the merits of each option.

Example criteria: "Initial investment," "ROI timeline," and "Regulatory challenges."

5. **Explore "what-If" scenarios:** Consider uncertainties or variables influencing outcomes. Add branches for scenarios like market changes or unexpected risks. **Example scenarios:** "What if demand drops?" "What if competition intensifies?"

6. **Prioritize objectivity:** Focus on evidence and data rather than assumptions or biases. Seek diverse perspectives to challenge the assumptions.

7. **Assess the best path ahead:** Compare options using the mapped-out consequences, criteria, and scenarios. Use the tree to identify the most logical and beneficial choice. **Example:** Select the option with the highest ROI and least risk based on analysis.

8. **Reflect on lessons:** After implementing the decision, revisit the tree to evaluate its effectiveness. Note any gaps or oversights to refine your decision-making process for the future.

Logic Tree vs. Decision Tree

Now, you may wonder what the difference between a logic tree and a decision tree is. The main distinction lies in that a logic tree helps you visualize the problem better and may not be as helpful in determining a solution. On the other hand, a decision tree, as its name suggests, will help you narrow down an outcome or choice logically.

Aspect	Logic Tree	Decision Tree
Focus	Breaking down problems logically.	Mapping decisions and outcomes.
Outcome	Deeper understanding of an issue.	Logically select a recommended decision or action.
Includes probabilities?	No	Yes

| Application | Analysis and exploration. | Decision making under uncertainty. |

VI Emerging Technology

Emerging technologies are reshaping education, work, and skill development, offering innovative tools to cultivate critical thinking. Engaging people in varied and interactive ways, these technologies create opportunities for analyzing, synthesizing, and evaluating information more effectively.

- **Machine learning (ML)** facilitates the identification of patterns in vast datasets, supporting predictive reasoning and enabling users to make informed decisions based on trends. Similarly, Big Data Analytics empowers us to critically evaluate large datasets, extracting meaningful insights through evidence-based approaches.

- **Virtual reality (VR)** takes critical thinking to a new level by immersing users in simulated real-world scenarios. These experiential environments encourage people to problem-solve dynamically, testing strategies and learning from outcomes. Complementing VR, augmented reality (AR) overlays contextual information onto the physical world, enabling us to dissect complex problems in an interactive and engaging manner.

- **Blockchain technology** fosters trust and critical assessment of data authenticity. By ensuring transparency and immutability, blockchain empowers users to verify information and draw conclusions based on reliable data. In language and argument analysis, natural language processing (NLP) assists us in understanding nuanced arguments, analyzing biases, and fostering deeper comprehension.

- **Gamification tools** integrate decision-making challenges into interactive formats, motivating users to develop critical thinking skills through trial and error in risk-free environments. Meanwhile, collaborative platforms powered by AI enhance teamwork and critical evaluation by facilitating group problem solving, ensuring equitable participation, and encouraging diverse perspectives.

- Lastly, **digital twins**—virtual models of physical entities and people—offer safe environments for testing "what-if" scenarios. By allowing experimentation with variables in a simulated setting, digital twins cultivate foresight and strategic thinking in users.

Together, all these technologies help bridge theory and practice, thereby fostering an adaptive, analytical mindset.

VII Social Networking and Social Media

Social networking and social media can also play a pivotal role in enhancing critical thinking by exposing one to various perspectives and fostering analytical engagement. Through these platforms, you encounter a wide range of opinions, challenging you to analyze information critically and fact-check claims to separate truth from misinformation.

Collaborative problem solving becomes accessible as you connect with people across geographic boundaries, sharing insights and solutions in real time. This collective intelligence encourages nuanced thinking and mutual learning. Additionally, discussion forums and debates spark intellectual engagement, pushing participants to defend their viewpoints, question assumptions, and refine arguments.

Algorithms, when designed to counteract echo chambers, can further support critical thinking by exposing users to viewpoints they might not typically encounter. Real-time engagement with global issues and current events provides opportunities to practice timely evaluation and informed decision making, ensuring social media isn't just a tool for consumption but also for meaningful intellectual growth if used wisely.

VIII News in Technology

Technology serves as a powerful tool to reinforce critical thinking by providing opportunities for intellectual engagement. Through access to news and emerging issues, it exposes us to complex global challenges, encouraging us to consider multifaceted perspectives. This immersion fosters a deeper understanding and analysis of nuanced topics.

By emphasizing evidence-based reasoning, technology empowers one to seek credible sources, verify facts, and build well-founded arguments. Tools like simulations and interactive platforms promote scenario analysis, allowing individuals to explore "what-if" situations and evaluate potential outcomes critically. Resources like Coursera or edX incorporate quizzes, case studies, and peer-reviewed discussions that promote active engagement and critical evaluation of ideas.

Technology also highlights the global and social contexts of issues, broadening users' awareness of interconnected challenges. Presenting diverse viewpoints, modern technological tools expand perspectives and challenge cognitive biases, cultivating a well-rounded, analytical approach to problem solving.

IX Understanding AI

Artificial intelligence (AI) refers to the development of computer systems that can perform tasks typically requiring human intelligence. These tasks include learning from data, reasoning, problem solving, language processing, and decision making. AI systems, powered by technologies like ML, NLP, and neural networks, adapt and improve over time through experience and data analysis.

AI can significantly enhance critical thinking by acting as both a tool and a partner in learning and decision-making processes. Here's how:

- **Encouraging analytical skills:** AI systems can process and analyze vast amounts of information, presenting patterns, trends, and insights that challenge individuals to engage deeply with data and interpret findings critically.

- **Facilitating evidence-based reasoning:** AI-powered fact-checking and data verification tools help users assess the credibility of information, promoting logical, evidence-backed decision making.

- **Simulating real-world scenarios:** Through virtual models and "what-if" simulations, AI allows users to explore the consequences of various decisions, enhancing strategic thinking and problem-solving skills.

- **Personalized learning:** Adaptive AI tutors identify a learner's strengths and weaknesses, tailoring challenges to build critical thinking skills progressively.

- **Exposing biases:** AI systems, especially those designed for text and argument analysis, help users detect biases in information or their reasoning, fostering more balanced and objective thinking.

- **Collaborative problem solving:** AI-powered platforms facilitate teamwork by organizing information, providing insights, and encouraging different perspectives during group discussions.

By engaging with AI tools, we equip ourselves with more efficient ways to access and evaluate information and also get inspired to ask better questions, refine our reasoning, and develop innovative solutions to complex problems.

X Modern Tools

When reading the news, it's crucial to distinguish fact from fiction. Below are IFCN-accredited fact-checking sites that focus on various areas. The International Fact-Checking Network (IFCN) website, also listed, offers additional resources (*LibGuides*, n.d.).

- **AAP FactCheck (Australia):** Verifies factual accuracy in statements from politicians and public figures in news media.

- **RMIT ABC Fact Check (Australia):** Assesses the accuracy of public claims in debates by politicians, advocacy groups, and institutions.

- **Full Fact (UK):** Independent fact-checkers who counter misinformation and its harmful effects.

- **FactCheck.org (U.S.):** Examines the accuracy of statements from major U.S. political players through ads, debates, and speeches, promoting informed public understanding.

- **International Fact-Checking Network (IFCN):** Promotes global best practices in fact-checking, offers resources, and fosters collaboration among fact-checkers.

- **PolitiFact (U.S.):** Pulitzer-winning site uses the Truth-O-Meter to evaluate claims from political leaders and activists.

- **Snopes (U.S.):** Offers evidence-based investigations with transparent sourcing to encourage independent research.

With credible, evidence-based, fact-checking sources, readers can make informed decisions, challenge misinformation, and contribute to a more knowledgeable and discerning society. Embracing these resources strengthens our ability to engage critically with the world around us.

As we have glimpsed, technology offers immense potential to cultivate critical thinking by providing tools for data analysis, collaborative problem solving, and immersive learning experiences. It enhances accessibility to dissimilar viewpoints, encourages evidence-based reasoning, and allows for innovative "what-if" scenario testing. These capabilities empower individuals to analyze information critically, identify biases, and make informed decisions.

However, technology also has its drawbacks. The vast influx of information can lead to cognitive overload, making it challenging to discern credible sources from misinformation. Additionally, overreliance on algorithms may inadvertently reinforce biases or create echo chambers, limiting exposure to diverse perspectives.

In Practice

Now, Tim, from the beginning of this chapter, could have avoided buying the "miracle" drug if he had just paid a little more attention to verifying sources and researching the credibility of the influencer. His experience teaches him to look for unbiased expert reviews or scientific evidence. You, too, can learn from Tim to:

- **Evaluate evidence:** Seek data supporting the product's claims, such as clinical trials, instead of relying on anecdotal evidence.

- **Challenge assumptions**: Question why the claims seem too good to be true and explore alternative explanations.

- **Consider multiple perspectives**: Look at negative reviews and critiques to form a balanced view before making a decision.

Ultimately, while technology can serve as a powerful aid in developing a critically sound mindset, its benefits depend on mindful and intentional use. Striking a balance between leveraging its advantages and mitigating its risks is key to fostering true critical thinking.

In the next section of this book, we shall focus on logical fallacies, what they are, and how we can deliberately steer clear of them.

Key Takeaways

- Critical thinking frameworks like **5W2H and SCQA** provide structured approaches to break down problems, evaluate solutions, and make informed decisions. These systems help analyze situations comprehensively, highlight challenges, and create actionable plans for resolving them.

- **Logic** and **decision trees** enhance clarity and objectivity by visually mapping problems, solutions, and outcomes. They encourage systematic thinking, challenge assumptions, and test scenarios, enabling well-rounded decision making.

- **Emerging technologies such as ML, big data analytics, and AI-powered tools** revolutionize critical thinking by offering insights, enabling evidence-based reasoning, and simulating complex scenarios to test outcomes in real time.

- **Social media and networking platforms** promote critical thinking by providing access to multiple perspectives, encouraging fact-checking, and fostering collaboration. When used mindfully, they challenge biases and expand awareness of global and social contexts.

- **Modern fact-checking tools and AI applications** support informed decision making by verifying information authenticity, identifying patterns, and enabling scenario analysis, ensuring critical thinking is grounded in data and evidence.

1. How can I apply the 5W2H and SCQA analysis systems to improve my decision making process in daily life or work?

2. In what situations do I typically rely on a top-down or bottom-up approach, and how might switching between them improve my problem solving?

3. How comfortable am I with using tools like logic trees and decision trees to break down complex problems? What challenges might I face in structuring them effectively?

4. How can I leverage emerging technologies such as AI, ML, and big data analytics to enhance my critical thinking skills?

5. How do I currently engage with social media and news platforms? Am I actively seeking various perspectives, or do I tend to fall into echo chambers?

6. When faced with uncertainty or a complex issue, how often do I use scenario analysis or "what-if" thinking to evaluate potential outcomes?

7. What are some common biases or assumptions I may have, and how can I challenge them when making decisions?

8. How can I incorporate tools for fact-checking and evidence-based reasoning into my daily routine to improve the accuracy of the information I trust and share?

Section 2:

Introspection

Chapter 6:

The Clarity Code—Unmasking Logical Fallacies

Dwelling on the negative simply contributes to its power. — Shirley MacLaine

Jake is a short filmmaker who prides himself on being a hardworking, visionary leader. However, Jake unthinkingly always attributes his successes to his skills and efforts but blames failures on external factors.

Jake's team launches a new short film that goes viral. Jake takes full credit, telling his boss that his innovative ideas drove the success, even though his team worked tirelessly to execute the project. However, when a second film flops due to unclear messaging—caused by Jake's rushed approvals—he blames the junior staff for not understanding his vision. This erodes trust within his team, leading to low morale and resignations.

Jake's self-bias extends to his personal life. He insists that he is the more responsible partner, gaslighting his wife Sarah's contributions. When arguments arise, Jake accuses Sarah of being too critical and never acknowledges how his defensiveness fuels their conflicts.

Because Jake rarely admits fault, he resists self-reflection. When friends suggest he work on his communication skills or consider therapy, he dismisses them, claiming he's fine and others are too sensitive. This mindset prevents him from growing or addressing the underlying insecurities driving his behavior.

Jake's inability to recognize his self-bias complicates his life. At work, his team's declining trust and productivity risk his career. At home, his marriage is on the brink of collapse. Internally, he feels frustrated and misunderstood, unaware that his refusal to take accountability is a major source of his problems.

At the outset, it is clear that Jake is to blame for several problems he blames others for. However, why is he simply not able to see this clearly? Let us look at cognitive distortions in logical reasoning that might lead us all to become Jakes in our lives.

Biases and Fallacies

Cognitive biases and logical fallacies are systematic patterns of deviation from rational thinking. They shape how we perceive, process, and recall information, often leading to errors in judgment and decision making. While these mental shortcuts, or heuristics, help us make quick decisions, they can also distort reality. Below is an overview of common biases with examples (Cherry, 2024-a; Cherry, 2024-b).

Attentional Bias

This bias entails focusing excessively on specific aspects of an event while ignoring others. For example, a person with anxiety pays more attention to potential dangers in their environment, overlooking neutral or positive details.

Confirmation Bias

Here, a person seeks information that confirms preexisting beliefs while ignoring contradictory evidence. Think of someone who believes in astrology, who only notices events that align with their horoscope predictions.

Hindsight Bias

This is when you believe, after an event occurs, that it was predictable all along. For instance, after a stock market crash, someone claims they "knew it was going to happen."

Anchoring Bias

When a person relies heavily on the first piece of information encountered (the "anchor") rather than the subsequent and more accurate evidence, an anchoring bias occurs. A car salesperson shows an expensive model first to make the subsequent cars seem like better deals.

Misinformation Effect

When one is repeatedly exposed to misleading information, one's memory becomes less accurate. For instance, a witness's memory of a car accident might change after hearing a biased retelling of the event.

Actor-Observer Bias

Actor-observer bias occurs when you attribute your own actions to external factors but others' actions to internal traits. For example, you blame traffic for being late, but when someone else is late, you think they're irresponsible.

False Consensus Effect

This is overestimating how much others share your beliefs or behaviors. For instance, one may believe that everyone enjoys the same movies as they do.

Halo Effect

This is the common mistake of judging someone's entire character based on one positive trait, like assuming a physically attractive person is also intelligent and kind.

Self-Serving Bias

When people attribute successes to themselves and failures to external factors, this bias occurs. For example, taking credit for a work success but blaming the team for a failure.

Availability Heuristic

This is overestimating the likelihood of events based on how easily examples come to mind. For instance, after seeing a news article about plane crashes, you overestimate the dangers of flying.

Optimism Bias

When you believe that you are less likely to experience negative events, it is called optimism bias. For instance, you assume you won't face a car accident even though you frequently text while driving.

Functional Fixedness

This bias limits an object to its traditional use, and one refuses to use it in any other way. A person may struggle to use a book as a doorstop because they only see it as something to read.

The Dunning-Kruger Effect

This fallacy includes overestimating one's knowledge or abilities, especially when lacking competence. For example, a novice chess player boasts they can beat an expert.

Status Quo Bias

This fallacy is preferring things to remain the same and resisting change. For instance, you reject a better insurance plan because switching feels inconvenient.

Apophenia

This is the perception of patterns or connections in unrelated data. For example, one believes that random stock market fluctuations follow a hidden pattern.

Framing Effect

Here, one is influenced by how information is presented rather than the content itself. For instance, we see "90% fat-free" as healthier than "10% fat," when in reality, both mean the same thing.

While the above serves as examples of common cognitive biases you may have encountered, it is not an exhaustive list. You can check out an even longer list of biases listed alphabetically on websites such as The Decision Lab (2023).

Next, before we look at ways to overcome logical fallacies, let us also look at some of those unique biases that seem to have sprouted up from our increased use of the internet and web resources.

Common Online Logical Fallacies

Logical fallacies are reasoning errors that undermine the validity of arguments. These fallacies frequently distort information on social media and online platforms due to the brevity of posts, the pursuit of engagement, and the absence of editorial oversight. While online platforms have democratized the sharing of ideas, they often prioritize simplicity, emotional appeals, or sensationalism, creating a fertile ground for fallacious reasoning.

Below is an exploration of some common logical fallacies and why they occur online (*Evaluating Online Information*, 2024).

Ad Hominem

Social media often fosters a confrontational environment where undermining the credibility of an individual can seem like an effective shortcut to discredit their position. Personal attacks are easier to craft than well-reasoned rebuttals.

An ad hominem is attacking the person making the argument instead of addressing the argument itself. Example: "Why should we trust her opinion on climate change? She dropped out of college!" This diverts attention from the argument's validity and shifts the focus to irrelevant personal data, discouraging meaningful discussion.

False Dichotomy

Platforms like Twitter, now renamed X, limit detailed arguments, so users often resort to oversimplifying complex issues. Binary choices are also easier to understand and can provoke stronger emotional reactions.

A false dichotomy is presenting a situation as having only two choices, ignoring the possibility of alternatives. Example: "Either you support this policy, or you don't care about children's future." This fallacy forces readers into an oversimplified view of the issue, discouraging critical thinking about potential middle-ground solutions or alternative approaches.

Post Hoc, Ergo Propter Hoc

Correlation is often mistaken for causation in casual, unverified claims online, as users tend to connect events in ways that feel intuitively logical but lack supporting evidence.

This type of fallacy happens when people assume that because one event follows another, the first event must have caused the second. Example: "I drank herbal tea yesterday, and my cold was gone this morning. The tea cured me!" This leads to spreading misinformation, as people may adopt or believe in practices or ideas based on unverified causal links.

Slippery Slope

Social media thrives on sensationalism, where exaggerating outcomes can make a post more engaging or shareable. Fear-based narratives often resonate deeply with audiences.

A slippery slope fallacy occurs when one tries to argue that a minor action will inevitably lead to extreme and dire consequences without evidence to support the chain of events. Example: "If we allow AI to write essays, students will stop learning entirely, and society will lose its intellectual capacity." The slippery slope fallacy creates unnecessary panic and discourages balanced debate about risks and benefits.

Straw Man

Simplifying or distorting an opponent's arguments is a quick way to create viral "mic drop" moments, where one appears to win an argument without engaging with its actual substance.

A straw man fallacy is misrepresenting or oversimplifying an opponent's argument to make it easier to refute. Example: "People who want stricter environmental regulations just want to ban all cars and force everyone to ride bikes." This approach derails conversations and prevents a nuanced discussion of differing viewpoints.

Some main reasons why online forums propagate such fallacies are:

- **Brevity of content:** Platforms like X or TikTok prioritize short, catchy posts that leave little room for detailed arguments or explanations.

- **Emotional appeals:** Content designed to provoke outrage, fear, or agreement often relies on fallacies, as emotional arguments garner more engagement than logical reasoning.

- **Echo chambers:** Social media algorithms promote content that aligns with users' existing beliefs, reinforcing biases and discouraging exposure to well-rounded arguments.

- **Lack of accountability:** Unlike broadcast news organizations, which employ editors and fact-checkers, social media platforms like Facebook have minimal oversight, leaving the burden of identifying errors to the audience.

- **Attention economy:** Sensationalism and controversy drive clicks and shares, incentivizing creators to prioritize virality over accuracy.

Unlike traditional broadcast news, which undergoes rigorous fact-checking and editing, social media places the responsibility of evaluating content on the individual.

Identifying logical fallacies equips users with the tools to critically assess arguments, identify weak reasoning, and distinguish valid points from faulty claims. While a fallacy doesn't necessarily mean an argument's conclusion is wrong, it does indicate that the evidence provided is insufficient to prove the point.

In learning to spot these fallacies, you can better navigate the overwhelming sea of information online and make more informed choices about what to believe and share.

In Practice: Overcoming Logical Fallacies and Cognitive Biases

If you haven't realized it already, Jake's main problem was a self-serving bias, damaging his relationships, hindering his personal growth, and leading to professional setbacks.

As he gets wiser, he employs some of the tactics below:

- **Fact-checking and content moderation:** Before accepting any claim as truth, he verifies its accuracy using credible sources. He cross-references claims with reputable sources and avoids relying solely on viral or trending posts.

    - **Tip:** Fact-checking platforms like Snopes, FactCheck.org, or official databases can help you assess the validity of information. Many platforms now flag or moderate misleading content, but you should still apply due diligence. Also, diversify your sources by including perspectives from different backgrounds, cultures, and ideologies.

- **Inoculating against misinformation:** Inoculation theory suggests that exposing yourself to small doses of misinformation, along with counterarguments, builds resilience against future fallacies and biases. Jake is better prepared to identify and resist misinformation by understanding how it works.

- o **Tip:** Familiarize yourself with common logical fallacies and cognitive biases so you can recognize them when they are used.

- **Labeling fallacies and biases:** When Jake encounters a flawed argument or bias, he names it. Identifying fallacies as "ad hominem" or "confirmation bias" helps him detach from the emotion of the argument and focus on its logic.

  - o **Tip:** Keep a mental or written list of common fallacies and biases as a reference.

- **Media literacy:** Jake improves his media and information literacy. This involves learning to discern credible sources, recognize manipulative tactics, and understand how information is presented.

  - o **Tip:** Take courses or workshops on critical thinking and media literacy to build your analytical skills.

- **Read and research with biases and fallacies in mind:** Approach information with the default mindset that biases and fallacies might be present. Actively question whether the argument presented is logical, evidence-based, or free from manipulation.

  - o **Tip:** Ask yourself, "What assumptions are being made here?" and "Does this conclusion follow from the evidence?"

- **6. Evaluate the source of the information:** The credibility of the source plays a significant role in determining the reliability of the information. Look for sources that have a track record of accuracy, transparency, and expertise.

  - o **Tip:** Avoid anonymous or heavily biased sources. Peer-reviewed studies, official reports, and respected news outlets are generally more reliable.

- **Evaluate the motive behind the information:** Jake tries to understand why certain information is being shared and, thereby, identifies potential biases or agendas. He asks himself, "Is the goal to inform, persuade, or manipulate?"

- o **Tip:** Be skeptical of emotionally charged language or appeals designed to provoke a reaction rather than present facts. Ask yourself, "Who benefits if I believe or act on this information?"

- **There is always more than one perspective:** Jake actively seeks out opposing viewpoints to challenge his assumptions and expand his understanding.

- o **Tip:** Engage in respectful discussions with people holding different opinions to see issues from multiple angles.

- **Using EI to overcome bias and fallacies:** Jake uses emotional grounding and intelligence to help him recognize and regulate his emotions to make clearer, more rational decisions.

- o **Tip:** Pause and reflect before reacting emotionally to information. Ask yourself, "Am I reacting emotionally or rationally?"

Overcoming logical fallacies and cognitive biases is an ongoing process that requires vigilance, education, and self-awareness. Cultivating these strategies, you can create a mindset of critical thinking and intellectual humility, empowering you to discern fact from fiction and engage with information thoughtfully. Always remember truth often lies in the nuance, and the path to it requires deliberate effort.

In the next chapter, we shall look yet more closely at the world of fake news and related misinformation and how one can save themselves from it.

Key Takeaways

- **Cognitive biases and logical fallacies:** These deviations from rational thinking can prevent one from seeing the entire picture and can lead to drawing faulty conclusions that can lead to wrong decisions.

- **Online logical fallacies:** These fallacies result from online posts and information that are too brief or intended to sensationalize news.

- **Being aware of logical fallacies and cognitive biases and taking steps not to fall prey to it** are the only remedies against fake news and misinformation.

Action Steps

1. How do I evaluate the credibility of the information I encounter?

2. Am I aware of my own biases when processing information?

3. How do I respond to emotionally charged or manipulative content?

4. Do I seek multiple perspectives to challenge my assumptions?

Chapter 7:

Strategic Minds—Navigating Fake News, Disinformation, and Deep Fakes

The possibilities are numerous once we decide to act and not react. –George Bernard Shaw

David, a nurse, loves staying informed about current health practices. His social media feeds are filled with posts and articles about various and sometimes conflicting medical practices. For instance, while some posts claim that a routine-based approach will enable quick patient recovery, others claim that sticking to rigid routines may not always provide the best outcome. Each article, video, and meme he sees presents starkly different narratives, often using emotional language, seemingly reliable facts, and sensational headlines. David feels torn—he wants to form his own opinion, but the sheer volume of conflicting information leaves him more confused than ever.

David's confusion turns into frustration and distrust. He starts doubting all medical articles and self-touted expert opinions. Discussions about nursing strategies make him anxious because he fears people will see his confusion. At work, he has trouble collating and processing patient medical histories and treatment plans, and making decisions based on them. He always fears even a tiny error might prove fatal for the patient—a fear magnified by the content he often sees online. On the other hand, he is often criticized by senior nurses and doctors for always waiting for their approvals to administer routine medications—something he is authorized and qualified to do. The fast-paced environment he works in leaves him feeling mentally and emotionally exhausted. The mental strain of maneuvering through his daily tasks spills into his personal life, leaving him irritable and withdrawn from even friends and family members.

David's case is not an exaggeration. Many of us find it hard to perform routine functions based on the misinformation we see online. There are so many conflicting opinions on what we should eat, how we should exercise, and the medicines we ought to take, that it is easier not to do anything. Is there any real remedy for this, or is this something to be put up with in the modern world? These are just some of the questions we shall seek to answer.

Fake News and Its Impact on Critical Thinking

Fake news refers to deliberately false or misleading information presented as legitimate news, crafted to manipulate public perception. While it often mimics genuine journalism, it lacks credible sources and journalistic integrity. Its core traits—false content, manipulative intent, and emotional appeal—create significant challenges for individuals trying to think critically.

The emotional manipulation inherent in fake news exploits fear, anger, or excitement, impairing rational decision making. Sensational headlines and false content provoke immediate reactions, making readers more likely to share without verifying accuracy. This "virality over validity" phenomenon spreads falsehoods quickly, leaving critical analysis behind. Furthermore, fake news often lacks credible citations, relying on unverified claims that leave readers with fragmented or distorted information.

Various types of fake news amplify the problem. Fabricated content and misleading headlines blur the line between truth and fiction, while wrong contexts manipulate real events to serve hidden agendas. Impostor news sources mimic reputable outlets, eroding trust in legitimate journalism.

- **Satire or parody:** Content created for entertainment, often using humor or exaggeration to comment on real events. Examples include websites like *The Onion* or *The Babylon Bee*. While not intended to deceive, satire can confuse readers, who mistake it for legitimate news, especially if shared out of context without clear labeling.

- **Fabricated content:** Completely false stories designed to mislead readers. These articles often mimic real news formats to appear credible but contain entirely fictional information. Fabricated content can spread dangerous misinformation, leading to misguided actions or beliefs, especially on sensitive topics like health, politics, or public safety.

- **Misleading headlines:** Sensational or clickbait titles that misrepresent the article's actual content. While the body of the article may contain accurate information, the headline often exaggerates or distorts the main points to draw readers in. Many people only read headlines and form opinions based on incomplete or distorted information, perpetuating misunderstandings.

- **False context:** Genuine facts or images placed in a misleading or unrelated context. For instance, a photo from one event may be presented as evidence of an unrelated incident. This type of fake news can distort public perception of events, fueling false narratives.

- **Impostor news sources:** Fake websites or articles designed to look like reputable news organizations, complete with similar logos and layouts. These sources trick readers into trusting false information because they mimic the credibility of well-known outlets.

The consequences of the above are severe. Socially, fake news sows division by fueling misinformation-driven conflicts. Emotionally, it creates stress and confusion. Mentally, it hampers rational thinking by encouraging reaction over reflection. To combat fake news, you must develop media literacy, question sources, and prioritize validity over virality.

Deepfakes: A New Frontier in Misinformation

Deepfakes are AI-generated media—images, videos, or audio recordings—designed to convincingly imitate real people, often making them appear to say or do things they never did. Created using advanced ML algorithms, deepfakes combine and manipulate data to produce hyper-realistic but fabricated content.

The rise of deepfakes poses significant challenges in combating misinformation online. By presenting false information in a highly believable format, deepfakes can manipulate public opinion and spread propaganda. For instance, a deepfake video of a world leader making provocative statements could escalate geopolitical tensions or reduce trust in governments. Similarly, deepfake audio recordings could incriminate individuals falsely, causing reputational damage.

Beyond misinformation, deepfakes have been used for personal gain, such as defrauding individuals or influencing behaviors to benefit the creator. They've also been misused in harmful ways, such as creating non-consensual explicit content. However, not all applications of deepfakes are malicious either—some are used for entertainment, scientific research, or even assisting individuals who have lost their voice to hear themselves speak again.

Despite their potential for harm, deepfakes can sometimes be identified by digital artifacts, unnatural movements, or inconsistencies. Researchers and tech companies are developing AI tools to detect and counteract deepfakes. As these technologies evolve, public awareness and critical evaluation of digital media are essential to mitigate the negative impact deepfakes have on perceptions and trust.

Misinformation and Disinformation: Understanding the Difference

In the digital age, misinformation and disinformation have emerged as significant challenges to truth and trust. While they may seem similar, their distinctions lie in intent and impact.

Misinformation refers to false or inaccurate information shared without the intent to deceive. It often spreads unintentionally, driven by misunderstanding or lack of verification. For example, someone might share an outdated news article on social media, believing it to be current. Misinformation is frequently fueled by the speed of digital communication, where users share content without critically evaluating its accuracy.

Disinformation, on the other hand, is deliberately false information created and shared with the explicit intent to deceive or manipulate. Unlike misinformation, disinformation is intentionally fabricated or distorted, often for political, financial, or ideological purposes. Examples include a fake news story designed to tarnish a political opponent's reputation or propaganda aimed at swaying public opinion on controversial topics.

The spread of both misinformation and disinformation can erode trust in media, polarize societies, and influence decision making on a large scale. Recognizing this growing issue, legislative efforts in the United States have sought to combat its effects. A proposed American bill (*H.R.6971 - 117th Congress, 2021*) advocates for increased information and media literacy education, equipping individuals with the tools to critically evaluate content and recognize manipulation. Such measures aim to reduce the impact of misinformation and disinformation, creating a more informed and discerning society by promoting awareness and resilience among the public.

As efforts like the above continue, addressing misinformation and disinformation requires collaboration between governments, technology platforms, educators, and the public.

In Practice: Interventions to Keep Fake News, Deep Fakes, Misinformation, and Disinformation at Bay

For a moment, let us get back to David and his anxiety surrounding vast amounts of often-conflicting information pertaining to health and patient care. Henceforth, how can David make sense of it all and develop a more balanced approach to what he reads and views online?

The steps he can use are also the measures we should use in our day-to-day interactions with online content.

- **Use trusted sources:** We should rely on well-established news outlets with a reputation for accuracy and a history of correcting mistakes. While using academic sources, ensure articles are peer-reviewed and published in reputed journals. Direct statements or reports from non-partisan organizations or experts in the field could clarify details about laws, medicine, wellness, and current events.

- **Evaluate claims critically:** Always ask critical questions like, *Who is behind this information? What evidence supports it? Is this an opinion, or does it cite reliable data?* Checking if the source has an agenda could help us separate fact from spin.

- **Avoid echo chambers:** Following diverse opinions—both aligned with and opposed to one's initial beliefs—can help form a balanced understanding of the issue.

- **Look for fact-checking:** Before believing any sensational claim, consult fact-checking websites like Snopes, FactCheck.org, or reputable international organizations for context. Medical information can be verified through trusted sources such as WHO or national medical association websites.

- **Learn to recognize misinformation:** Signs like emotionally charged language, lack of credible citations, or claims that sound too extreme are red flags for fake or exaggerated news.

- **Set time limits:** We can always limit our time scrolling through social media and focus instead on consuming information in manageable doses from reliable sources.

- **The right action at the right time:** Lastly, based on the fact-based, relevant, and accurate information one has gathered, take the right action at the right time. Sometimes, like in David's case, inaction can also mean putting your own or another person's life in jeopardy, or being silently complicit in the evils spread via fake news.

Like David, we too can approach controversial topics with confidence, resist the emotional pull of misinformation, and make better-informed decisions by adopting these habits regularly and sticking to them.

Key Takeaways

- **Fake news** encompasses deliberately false or misleading content designed to deceive or manipulate.

- **Deepfakes** are AI-generated media that fabricate realistic visuals or audio, making it appear as though someone said or did something they didn't.

- **Misinformation** is false information shared unintentionally, while **disinformation** is deliberately fabricated to deceive or manipulate for personal, political, or ideological gain.

- Always check the credibility of sources, look for citations, and cross-reference information with trusted outlets.

Action Steps

1. How often do I verify the credibility of the information I consume or share, and what steps can I take to ensure its accuracy?

2. Am I aware of my emotional reactions to sensational headlines or media, and how might these reactions influence my judgment?

3. Do I engage critically with diverse perspectives, or do I tend to stay within an echo chamber that reinforces my existing beliefs?

Chapter 8:

The Decision Matrix—Negotiating Algorithmic Influence

By their very nature, heuristic shortcuts will produce biases, and that is true for both humans and artificial intelligence... –Daniel Kahneman

Samantha is a mom with a packed schedule and a penchant for efficiency. She loves exploring new places to eat, often relying on online reviews and social media for recommendations. Samantha considers herself discerning but also trusts influencers and reviewers who appear knowledgeable, as she doesn't have the time to fact-check everything herself.

She comes across a viral post on Instagram from "FoodieExpert," an account she has followed for months due to its polished food photography and confident critiques. The post harshly criticizes a newly opened café in her neighborhood, claiming unsanitary conditions and showing a blurry photo of a messy counter. Samantha, drawn in by the dramatic tone and her past trust in the account, quickly decides to cross the café off her list without further investigation. Eager to save her friends from a bad experience, she shares the post with her network, unintentionally amplifying the negative review.

Samantha's reliance on the authority heuristic—trusting the opinion of someone who appears to be an expert—leads to unintended consequences. The café, struggling as a new business, suffers from a sudden drop in customers due to the viral post. When Samantha learns later that the photo was misleading and the review fabricated by a rival café owner, she feels guilty and embarrassed for contributing to the harm. Her friends start questioning her recommendations, and Samantha begins to doubt her judgment.

Many of us, like Samantha, are quick to share information from people who brand themselves "experts." While the benefit of modern technology is its lightning speed, this could also be a disadvantage when it comes to propagating false information.

Apart from not verifying the facts fully, Samantha made the mistake of relying on her "intuition," which is a part of the mental shortcuts that all of us adopt as we become more experienced in life. Let us look at these mental shortcuts or heuristics, their necessity, and their pros and cons.

Heuristics: Mental Shortcuts in Decision Making

Heuristics are cognitive strategies or mental shortcuts that help individuals make quick decisions and judgments without extensive deliberation. These rules-of-thumb streamline problem solving and probability assessments, especially in situations where time or information is limited. While heuristics can be beneficial, they can also impede critical thinking, leading to errors in reasoning.

One of the primary advantages of heuristics is their ability to reduce cognitive load. For instance, while grocery shopping, a person might choose a product with the label "best seller" instead of comparing every available option. This availability heuristic, where decisions are based on readily recalled information, can save time and effort. Similarly, the representativeness heuristic—judging the likelihood of an event based on how similar it seems to a known stereotype—can provide quick approximations in unfamiliar situations.

However, reliance on heuristics often comes at the expense of accuracy. These mental shortcuts can lead to biases and irrational conclusions. Confirmation bias, for instance, causes people to seek information that supports their existing beliefs while ignoring contradictory evidence. Similarly, the authority heuristic may prompt individuals to trust experts or influencers without critically evaluating their claims, as seen in the spread of misinformation.

To balance the utility of heuristics with critical thinking, individuals must develop awareness of their cognitive shortcuts. Pausing to evaluate decisions, question assumptions, and seek diverse perspectives can mitigate the pitfalls of heuristics. While heuristics offer efficiency, integrating mindful and deliberate reasoning ensures more informed and rational decision making.

Let us look at how the negative impact of heuristics can be compounded by online tools like social media and social networking platforms.

Social Media Algorithms: The Power Behind Your Feed

Social media algorithms are the invisible engines that curate and prioritize content on platforms like Facebook, Instagram, and Twitter. These algorithms analyze user data—such as likes, shares, and browsing history—to personalize the user experience, ensuring that individuals see content most relevant to their interests. While these algorithms enhance user engagement and make platforms more enjoyable, they also have significant implications for critical thinking and information consumption.

Why Do We Need Algorithms?

Given the massive amount of content generated on social media daily, algorithms help sift through the noise to present users with what they're most likely to find engaging. Without algorithms, users would be overwhelmed by irrelevant posts and endless streams of unfiltered information.

Algorithms personalize and tailor content to individual preferences, making social media browsing more efficient and enjoyable. For example, a food enthusiast may primarily see recipe videos and restaurant recommendations. Algorithms help platforms maintain user interest and build vibrant online communities by showing content users are likelier to interact with.

Despite these advantages, algorithms also come with some disadvantages, such as the following:

- **Echo chambers and confirmation bias**: Algorithms often create "echo chambers," where users are exposed to information that aligns with their existing beliefs. For instance, a user with strong political opinions may only see content supporting those views, reinforcing confirmation bias and skewing their perception of reality.

- **Engagement over accuracy:** To maximize engagement, platforms prioritize sensational or emotionally charged content, which can overshadow factual accuracy. For example, a provocative but misleading headline may be promoted over a well-researched article simply because it sparks more reactions.

- **Limited exposure to varied opinions:** Filtering content based on user preferences and algorithms restricts access to opposing viewpoints. This makes it harder to understand complex issues from multiple angles and promotes polarized discussions.

- **Fast-paced consumption:** The rapid flow of algorithm-driven content discourages users from pausing to analyze information critically. A user scrolling through dozens of posts in seconds is unlikely to fact-check or deeply evaluate each piece of content.

Since social media algorithms wield significant influence over what we see and how we think, understanding their benefits and drawbacks sets us up to reclaim control over our digital experiences.

We shall now explore critical thinking and its power in nurturing a more balanced and critical perspectives irrespective of heuristics and algorithms.

In Practice: Mitigating Heuristics and Algorithmic Biases—Strengthening Critical Thinking

Going back to Samantha's reliance on "expert" opinion, she can easily avoid a similar episode from repeating if she:

- **Takes time to verify:** Allocate a few minutes to look up other reviews or check platforms like Yelp or Google for balanced opinions.

- **Questions the "expert":** Does the account have real credibility, or does it rely on aesthetic appeal and confident language to gain trust?

- **Avoids snap judgments:** Visit the café to form a personal opinion instead of relying solely on hearsay.

- **Thinks critically about emotional content:** Observe exaggerated language and blurry photos, pause, and consider whether a post is trustworthy.

In an age where social media algorithms and cognitive shortcuts shape much of our decision making, boosting our critical thinking is essential. Individuals can make more informed judgments and avoid the pitfalls of bias and misinformation by recognizing and addressing these influences. The following are some easy steps we can follow:

Recognize Algorithmic Influence

Social media algorithms prioritize engagement, often reinforcing confirmation bias by showing content similar to previous interactions. To counter this, ask why specific posts or ads appear in your feed. Consider who benefits from your engagement. Similarly, recognize that algorithms often prioritize sensational content, not accuracy.

Identify Cognitive Biases

Cognitive biases like confirmation bias, the bandwagon effect, and the availability heuristic can distort critical thinking. You can reduce their impact by seeking diversity. Actively explore information that challenges your views, and exercise self-awareness in consciously reflecting on how biases influence your decisions and judgments.

Practice Skepticism

Adopt a skeptical mindset to evaluate content critically. Check sources and verify the credibility of sources and use fact-checking tools, some of which we have already discussed in the previous chapters. Scrutinize intent and question the authenticity and purpose behind the content before accepting or sharing it.

Slow Down Reactions

Emotional responses can lead to hasty decisions. Combat this by pausing before reacting. Reflect on the content's accuracy, intent, and context. Next, Avoid clickbait. Resist your natural tendency to react to provocative headlines without verifying their claims.

Broaden Perspectives

Breaking out of algorithm-driven echo chambers requires some effort. Ensure you follow diverse voices. Deliberately chat or discuss topics with accounts and groups offering alternative viewpoints. Also, engage in respectful dialogues with people who hold different opinions.

Leverage Tools and Settings

Finally, take full control of your online environment. You can customize feeds and switch to chronological feeds to reduce the algorithmic influence. You can also analyze bias using several tools available online, which highlight bias in media and platforms. Use them to ensure a balanced information exposure.

These strategies can negate the effects of heuristics and algorithms, allowing you to fully exercise your critical thinking to navigate the modern information landscape effectively.

In the next chapter, we look at being critically attuned to the personality we project online in terms of the personal information we willingly or unwillingly share online and the digital footprint we leave behind.

Key Takeaways

- **Heuristics save time but can mislead:** Mental shortcuts simplify decision making but may result in biases like confirmation bias or the availability heuristic, leading to inaccurate conclusions.

- **Algorithms tailor content but reinforce echo chambers:** Social media algorithms prioritize personalized and engaging content, often limiting exposure to multiple perspectives and reinforcing preexisting beliefs.

- **Critical Thinking is essential:** Recognizing algorithmic influence and cognitive biases allows you to question content, seek alternative viewpoints, and evaluate information more effectively.

- **Pause and reflect before reacting:** Slowing down reactions to emotionally charged content can help mitigate the impulsive spread of misinformation.

- **Take control of your online experience:** Use tools like fact-checkers, chronological feeds, and diverse content sources to counter the negative impacts of algorithms and heuristics.

Action Steps

1. **Question your digital environment:**

   a. Look at your social media feed for 10 minutes and note the type of content you see.

   b. Ask yourself:

      i. Why am I seeing this content?

      ii. Is it reinforcing my existing beliefs?

      iii. Who benefits from my engaging with this content?

2. **Identify your biases:**

   a. Think about a recent decision or belief you formed based on online content.

   b. Now reflect on these questions:

      i. Did I accept the information without questioning it?

      ii. Could confirmation bias or the availability heuristic have influenced my judgment?

        iii. Did I seek out alternative perspectives before forming an opinion?

3. **Evaluate a viral post:**

    a. Choose a viral post or trending topic from social media.

    b. Investigate its source and cross-check the claims with reputable sources.

    c. Ask:

        i. Is this post emotionally charged or sensationalized?

        ii. How does the intent of the content creator align with factual accuracy?

4. **Expand your perspectives:**

    a. Follow three accounts that offer viewpoints different from your own.

    b. After a week, reflect:

        i. How did this exposure challenge or enrich my understanding of a topic?

        ii. Did I notice biases in my initial reactions to their content?

5. **Pause before sharing:**

    a. Recall a time you shared or reacted to online content impulsively.

    b. Reflect:

        i. What motivated my reaction?

        ii. Could pausing have changed how I interpreted or shared the information?

        iii. How might I approach similar situations differently in the future?

Chapter 9:

Digital Shadows—Managing Online Identity

You are what you share. –C.W. Leadbeater

Emma was a young accountant with a passion for photography. Her Instagram was filled with stunning landscapes, candid moments, and a glimpse into her personal life. She often tagged her favorite coffee shop, shared real-time updates about her weekend getaways, and mentioned her workplace in passing. On LinkedIn, Emma proudly shared her career milestones and hinted at her daily schedule.

Emma didn't realize that these seemingly innocent tidbits created a detailed digital map of her life.

She felt uneasy when she noticed a stranger frequently commenting on her posts, referencing details she had casually mentioned—like her dog's name and her love for late-night runs. At first, she brushed it off, but then she started receiving personalized messages. This person even showed up at her favorite coffee shop and tried to strike up a conversation, claiming they ' knew" her.

Terrified, Emma stopped posting for weeks. But the damage had been done. The stranger called her workplace and pretended to know her personally. Eventually, she had to involve the police to address what had become a stalking situation.

The experience left Emma shaken. She learned the hard way that small breadcrumbs of information, spread across platforms, can be pieced together by anyone. The experience taught Emma to be cautious—avoid geotags, limit personal details, and ensure her privacy settings were airtight.

Emma's case is not one out of the blue. Many of us might have experienced less scary but disturbing episodes of being "chatted up" by random strangers. While most of these messages can be ignored or blocked, putting an end to them, there is always the chance our profiles may catch the attention of a malicious and deliberate cyber stalker.

In this chapter, we look at what digital footprints are and how to ensure online safety and security.

Critically Managing Your Online Presence and Staying Safe

Your online presence serves as your digital footprint. Managing yourself online is more than just a good idea; it's a necessity. Your digital footprint can impact your privacy, security, professional reputation, and even how others perceive you. Taking deliberate steps to critically evaluate and improve your online presence can help you stay safe while maintaining control over your personal narrative.

Let us try to craft a guide to critically assess and present your online persona smartly.

How Much Information Do You Leave Online?

Every interaction you make online leaves a trail of information about you. This can include:

- **Social media posts:** photos, updates, check-ins, and shared links

- **Profiles and biographies:** public-facing profiles on LinkedIn, Instagram, X, or Facebook

- **Interactions:** comments, likes, and participation in forums or online communities

- **Purchases and registrations:** information from e-commerce sites, newsletters, and apps

- **Search histories:** items you search online that are tracked and logged by browsers and search engines

Individually, these tidbits may seem insignificant, but when combined, they create a detailed profile that could be exploited by malicious people, advertisers, or even curious strangers.

So, how do we manage digital DNA that we may unwittingly leave behind?

Steps to Critically Manage Your Online Presence

Search Your Name Online

Use search engines like Google to look up your name, email address, usernames you use on sites, and phone number. Include variations, nicknames, and maiden names. Ask yourself: What appears in the search results? Are there images, comments, or old accounts that you forgot about? Does any of the information compromise your privacy or professional image?

The answers will give you an idea of reviewing your accounts.

Review Social Media Accounts

Audit all your social media accounts, even the ones you rarely use. Pay special attention to:

- **Privacy settings:** Set profiles to private where possible and restrict content to trusted connections.

- **Old content:** Review and delete outdated posts, photos, and comments that might no longer reflect your values or could be misinterpreted.

- **Tagged content:** Remove yourself from photos or posts where you've been tagged without consent.

Check for Data Leaks

Use online tools like *Have I Been Pwned* to see if your email or other data has been compromised in breaches. If you suspect any leaks, change your passwords immediately. You can use a password manager to create and store strong, unique passwords for every account. Lastly, enable two-factor authentication (2FA) on all accounts to add an extra layer of security.

Analyze Linked Accounts

Many apps and platforms offer sign-in options using social media or email accounts. Review these connections to understand:

- which accounts or apps are linked to your main email or social media profiles.

- what permissions these linked accounts have.

- whether any of these services are unnecessary or pose a risk to your data security.

Finally, disconnect or, if possible, deactivate any accounts you no longer use or trust.

Examine Permissions

You can review the permissions granted to apps on your devices. Some permissions are unnecessary and invasive. For example, does a flashlight app need access to your location? Does a game need access to your microphone or contacts?

Restrict permissions to only what is essential for the app's functionality. This way you won't share personal details where it is unnecessary.

Engage in Social Media "Googling"

Use the "View As" tool available on many platforms (e.g., Facebook's "View As Public" feature) to see your profile from the perspective of a stranger. Scrutinize the following:

- photos, posts, or personal details are visible to the public

- whether there is any content that could be misused or taken out of context

- how your profile aligns with the image you want to project

Next, let us look at why these elaborate steps need to be taken at all.

Why Online Safety Matters

Privacy Protection

Sensitive information like your home address, phone number, or financial details can be exploited for identity theft, fraud, or even stalking. Limiting public exposure minimizes these risks.

Professional Reputation

Employers, clients, and colleagues often research potential candidates or partners online. A polished, professional digital presence can help you stand out, while inappropriate content can harm your credibility or make you look indecisive or even stupid.

Social Perception

Your online activity shapes how friends, family, and the broader community perceive you. Even innocent posts can be taken out of context or misunderstood and create a lot of damage and hurt.

Data Security

Platforms collect and store vast amounts of user data. Understanding their policies and practices helps you ensure that your information isn't being misused or sold.

Control Over Personal Narrative

By carefully managing what you share, you control how you are portrayed online, ensuring it aligns with your values, beliefs, and goals.

At this juncture, you may have a very valid concern. If online engagement is so dangerous, why don't I just delete all my accounts and stay safe? Well, let us critically weigh the pros and cons of being active online.

The Pros and Cons of Online Engagement

Yays	Nays
Networking opportunities: Platforms like LinkedIn and industry-specific forums enable you to connect with professionals and mentors, which can prove a blessing for your career growth.	**Privacy risks:** Oversharing can expose you to identity theft, phishing scams, or even physical danger.
Staying in touch: In this busy world, social networking enables us to stay connected to friends and family members who may no longer be near enough to visit or call regularly.	**Reputational harm:** Old posts, insensitive comments, or misunderstood humor can come back to haunt you.
Creative and professional showcases: Social media can be a great platform to display your work, from portfolios to personal projects.	**Data exploitation:** Social media platforms often share user data with advertisers or third parties without explicit consent, which means our information is being used by companies for advertising and pushing products.
Access to resources and communities: Many platforms offer free educational content, support groups, and networking events.	**Time drain:** Engaging with social media excessively can be distracting and unproductive, even leading to insomnia, depression, and anxiety.

Staying informed: Social media provides real-time updates on news and trends relevant to your interests.	

From the facts above, one thing emerges clearly—when used right, the benefits of social media engagement outweigh its negatives.

Next, let us look at how social media has policies built in for our safety and how we can leverage them more effectively.

Social Media Policies and Your Information

- **Review terms of service:** Take time to read the terms of service for the platforms you use. These documents outline how your data is collected, stored, and shared.

- **Data ownership:** Understand whether you retain ownership of the content you upload or if the platform claims rights to use it for their purposes.

- **Data deletion options:** Look into the platform's policies for deleting accounts and data. Some services allow you to deactivate your account but still retain your data.

- **Third-party sharing:** Many platforms share your data with advertisers, analytics firms, and other third parties. Knowing this can help you make informed decisions about which platforms to trust.

Your digital footprint is an extension of yourself. Being mindful and proactive ensures that it reflects the best version of who you are while keeping you safe from potential threats. Start taking control of your online presence today and reap the benefits of a secure, polished, and professional digital identity.

Key Takeaways

Online safety is a big part of the narrative you craft for yourself. This can be managed with a few simple steps such as:

- Reviewing how much information you leave online and changing your habits where needed.

- Checking privacy and third-party policies of social media sites and changing the settings to maximize the security of your profile.

- Cross-checking the "permissions" granted to particular apps on your devices so that unscrupulous elements can't access unnecessary details about you.

Action Steps

1. How much of my digital presence is intentional versus accidental?

2. Have I ever considered how my online activity could affect my personal or professional life in the future?

3. If someone searched for me online, what would they find? Does this align with the image I want to present?

4. When I interact online, am I contributing to meaningful and respectful conversations?

5. Have I considered how my current online activity could be interpreted by different audiences (e.g., employers, family, friends)?

Section 3:
Critical Thinking Growth

Chapter 10:

Mental Models—Frameworks for Better Thinking

Responsibility to yourself means refusing to let others do your thinking, talking, and naming for you; it means learning to respect and use your own brains and instincts; hence, grappling with hard work. –Adrienne Rich

Tara, a campaign developer, is tasked with launching an ad for a high-profile client. She juggles numerous responsibilities—managing her team, coordinating with the client, and overseeing the creative and logistical aspects of the campaign. Under pressure to deliver results quickly, Tara jumps straight into action without much forethought.

She immediately assigns tasks to her team based on availability rather than expertise and prioritizes whatever seems urgent. As deadlines approach, the team encounters repeated miscommunications, duplication of effort, and missed opportunities to innovate. The client is dissatisfied with the lackluster campaign, and Tara feels burned out, blaming her team for their inefficiency.

Tara's struggle stems from her failure to employ higher-order thinking skills (HOTS) in Bloom's Taxonomy, especially analysis, evaluation, and creativity. Reacting impulsively and bypassing structured planning and critical thinking, she has limited her ability to anticipate challenges, align her team, or explore innovative ideas.

So what could Tara and we do to employ HOTS and make it part of our regular thinking? This chapter will outline a variety of methods that we can use individually and in tandem to elevate our thinking capacities.

Let us explore seven ways in which critical thinking and higher-order thinking can be boosted.

Brainstorming

Brainstorming is a collaborative problem-solving technique used to generate a wide range of ideas in a short amount of time. It encourages creativity by allowing individuals or groups to think freely and share thoughts without fear of judgment.

The primary goal of brainstorming is to explore possibilities, solutions, or strategies for a specific problem, question, or goal. Unlike structured decision making, it emphasizes quantity over quality during the initial phase, with the belief that even unconventional or seemingly impractical ideas can inspire valuable insights. Let us look at some great ways to maximize output during brainstorming (*What is brainstorming?*, 2016):

Start by **setting a time limit**, typically 15–60 minutes, depending on the problem's complexity. This constraint helps participants focus their energy and prevents fatigue. Begin with a clearly defined problem or goal, so the group has a shared understanding of what they are tackling, ensuring that ideas stay on topic.

One of the cornerstones of effective brainstorming is the **absence of judgment or criticism**. No criticism or evaluation occurs during idea generation. Participants should feel safe to share their ideas without fear of negative reactions, verbal or nonverbal. Weird and unconventional ideas are not only welcomed but encouraged, as they can spark innovative solutions and prevent groupthink.

Quantity matters—more ideas lead to a higher likelihood of uncovering quality solutions. Sifting through ideas and refining them can come later. Participants should also build on each other's contributions, using a mindset of "and" rather than "but" to expand and evolve ideas into new insights.

Staying visual by using diagrams or Post-Its can help make abstract concepts tangible and spark fresh perspectives.

Finally, **allowing one conversation at a time** ensures respect for everyone's input and keeps the discussion focused on generating actionable results.

The same principles above can be used if you were to brainstorm solutions to a problem all on your own. In other words, focus on wild ideas and as many of them as you can think up. Don't be critical or hard on yourself and try to put your ideas visually in a notepad or digital document. Ensure you entertain and focus on one idea at a time, teasing out all its possibilities before moving to the next one.

Six Hats Thinking

The Six Thinking Hats method, developed by Edward de Bono in the 1980s, is a structured approach to thinking that helps individuals and groups analyze issues from multiple perspectives. It encourages participants to "wear" metaphorical hats, each representing a distinct mode of thinking, to focus their attention and improve decision making (Hancock, 2024).

This method reduces biases, encourages creativity, and fosters balanced problem solving by deliberately adopting different viewpoints.

Let us look at the six Hats, the types of questions we need to ask while wearing each hat, and the objective of doing so.

The Six Hats and Their Questions

1. **White hat (Relying on facts and information):** Here, we aim to focus on data, facts, and objective information, avoiding emotions or opinions.

    o **Questions:** What information do we have? What are the facts? What do we need to know? How can we find the missing information?

2. **Red hat (Encouraging emotions and feelings):** Acknowledge emotions and instinctive responses without requiring justification.

    o **Questions:** How do I feel about this? What is my gut instinct? Are there any intuitive reactions or concerns?

3. **Black hat (Accepting critical judgment):** Identify weaknesses, challenges, and potential flaws to minimize risks.

   o **Questions:** What are the potential risks or downsides? What could go wrong? Why might this fail?

4. **Yellow hat (Fostering optimism and benefits):** Highlight the positive aspects and opportunities to encourage a constructive outlook.

   o **Questions:** What are the benefits? Why is this idea valuable? How could this succeed?

5. **Green hat (Nurturing creativity and innovation):** Promote creativity and generate innovative solutions or approaches.

   o **Questions:** What new ideas or solutions can we explore? How can we think outside the box? What alternatives exist?

6. **Blue hat (Regulating process and control):** Manage the thinking process, ensure focus, and maintain the agenda during discussions.

   o **Questions:** What is our goal? What is the next step? Are we staying on track?

A great method to troubleshoot business strategy, education, conflict resolution, and personal choices, the Six Hats method improves balanced thinking, creativity, collaboration, clear decision making, and efficient communication.

Design Thinking Exercises

Design thinking is a human-centered approach to innovation and problem solving that prioritizes empathy, creativity, and practicality. It seeks to understand user needs deeply, define clear problems, ideate innovative solutions, and refine them through prototyping and testing. This iterative process ensures that the final product or service is both effective and user-focused (SEI TEAM, 2023; *The Best Design Thinking Exercises,* 2022).

The Design Thinking Process

1. **Empathize:** This step involves stepping into the user's shoes to understand their motivations, challenges, and unmet needs. By questioning assumptions and analyzing behaviors in the context of a dynamic world, businesses can uncover insights to anticipate future needs.

2. **Define:** Clearly articulate the problem statement by synthesizing user insights and leveraging existing organizational knowledge and capabilities. This stage transforms abstract observations into actionable focus points.

3. **Ideate:** Brainstorm and generate creative solutions, considering both customer value and feasibility. Encouraging out-of-the-box thinking helps prioritize impactful ideas that can drive meaningful change.

4. **Prototype:** Create tangible representations of solutions to visualize their potential. Iterating on prototypes allows teams to refine functionality, gather feedback, and achieve alignment before investing significant resources in development.

5. **Test:** Test solutions in real-world scenarios through trial phases. This stage ensures usability and fine-tunes the design to meet customer expectations, ultimately delivering an exceptional user experience.

Design thinking can employ several types of exercises depending on the problem at hand and the amount of time you have to bring a solution. Let us explore a few of these:

- **Rapid prototyping:** Teams quickly create low-fidelity models (like sketches, mock-ups, or simple builds) to visualize ideas. This enables early testing and feedback, preventing costly missteps.

- **Empathy mapping:** Teams chart what users say, think, feel, and do using visual maps. This tool helps align designs with user needs and emotions and ensures solutions are grounded in the user's perspective.

- **SCAMPER:** This is a brainstorming technique where teams explore innovations by modifying an existing product or idea using prompts like "Substitute," "Combine," "Adapt," "Modify," "Put to another use," "Eliminate," and "Reverse." For example, rethinking a product's packaging to serve a dual purpose could emerge from SCAMPER.

- **Role-playing:** Thinkers themselves act as end-users, simulating interactions with a product, idea, or service. This builds empathy and uncovers usability issues.

- **Dot voting/note and vote:** Teams generate and share ideas on sticky notes, then vote with dots to identify the most promising ones. This democratizes decision making.

- **Affinity grouping:** Ideas or data are categorized into broader themes or patterns to identify patterns and prioritize efforts. This is particularly useful for synthesizing insights during brainstorming sessions.

Design thinking combines creativity, empathy, and analysis to solve complex problems effectively, making it widely applicable in industries such as technology, healthcare, education, and beyond.

Mind Mapping

A mind map is a powerful tool for organizing thoughts visually, using a central idea as the starting point and branching out with related concepts, ideas, or tasks. It's a flexible method for capturing, organizing, and expanding your thinking, combining visuals with logical connections to enhance comprehension and recall.

At its core, a mind map mirrors how your brain naturally processes information. It begins with a central idea, drawn as a circle or a node, from which branches radiate outward. Each branch represents a subtopic or key idea, often labeled with keywords, phrases, or images. These branches can then extend further into sub-branches, forming a web of interconnected ideas.

For instance:

- Central Idea: "World War II"

- o   Branches: Causes, Key Events, Leaders, Impacts
- o   Sub-branches: (under "Key Events") D-Day, Battle of Britain, Pearl Harbor, etc.

The format taps into your brain's natural preference for associations and visualization, making complex ideas easier to grasp.

Mind mapping offers numerous benefits, particularly in enhancing HOTS. It encourages analysis by breaking down complex ideas into smaller, manageable parts and encourages evaluation through the ability to compare and connect concepts.

How to Mind Map

1. **Start with a central idea:** Place your main concept in the center of a blank page. Use a bold word or image to represent it.

2. **Add main branches:** Think of the major categories or key aspects related to the central idea. Use a different color for each branch.

3. **Expand with sub-branches:** For each main branch, add smaller branches with more specific ideas, details, or examples.

4. **Use keywords and images:** Keep the text minimal and focus on strong keywords. Add icons, doodles, or symbols for visual appeal.

5. **Keep it dynamic:** Mind maps aren't static. They can evolve as you discover new connections or ideas.

6. **Review and refine:** After creating your mind map, look for patterns or areas that need additional depth.

Combining logic and creativity, mind maps engage both sides of the brain, boosting memory and recall through their visual and associative nature. They improve problem solving and decision making by allowing users to visualize all aspects of a challenge, facilitating innovative solutions. Additionally, mind maps promote creativity by encouraging connections between seemingly unrelated ideas and enhance collaboration by providing a clear and participatory framework for team projects.

Spaced Repetition

Spaced repetition is a learning technique that involves reviewing information at increasing intervals over time. Rooted in cognitive psychology, it leverages the spacing effect—a phenomenon where information is better retained when reviewed periodically rather than crammed in a single session (Frank, 2020). Aligning with how memory works, spaced repetition helps deepen understanding and paves the way for advanced critical thinking.

Spaced repetition is not just about memorization—it lays the groundwork for higher-order thinking by solidifying foundational knowledge and enabling its application in complex scenarios. Here's how:

- **Analysis:** Retention of critical facts and concepts enables one to break down and dissect complex ideas more effectively.

- **Synthesis:** With solid recall, individuals can integrate previously learned ideas into new contexts, boosting creativity and innovation.

- **Evaluation:** Consistently revisiting and refining knowledge helps assess its relevance and validity, strengthening decision making and critical reasoning.

By creating a robust knowledge base, spaced repetition allows you to move beyond rote learning to more sophisticated applications, such as solving problems, forming connections, and generating new insights.

How Spaced Repetition Works

The method is simple but powerful:

1. **Initial learning:** Study new material and grasp its basics.

2. **Revisit strategically:** Review it shortly after the first exposure, then again after longer intervals (e.g., after a day, a week, then a month).

3. **Adjust intervals:** Over time, as retention improves, extend the intervals between reviews.

Tools like flashcards, apps like Anki and Quizlet, or digital calendars are commonly used to implement spaced repetition effectively.

An example of space repetition would look like this: Imagine a student is preparing for a history exam and needs to remember the key events of World War II. They could create a schedule like this:

1. **Day 1:** Learn key events like the invasion of Poland, the Battle of Britain, and D-Day.

2. **Day 2:** Review the material briefly, focusing on details they struggled to recall on Day 1.

3. **Day 7:** Revisit the events, this time including their causes and outcomes.

4. **Day 30:** Conduct a final review, integrating all details into a timeline to reinforce connections.

By spacing reviews, an individual moves the information from short-term to long-term memory, enabling them to analyze relationships (e.g., causes and effects), synthesize insights (e.g., patterns across battles), and evaluate their significance in shaping history.

In academic learning, this method is ideal for mastering subjects like mathematics, history, or language vocabulary, where one builds on foundational knowledge. It also aids skill development, particularly in acquiring technical skills such as coding or medical procedures, which require a combination of theoretical understanding and practical application. Spaced repetition can help retain material over the long-term, making it invaluable for competitive exams like the SATs, GRE, or professional certifications. Additionally, it supports continuous learning in professional fields such as law, engineering, and medicine, where concepts constantly evolve and require regular reinforcement.

Active Recall

Active recall is a learning technique that involves actively retrieving information from memory rather than passively reviewing material (Beckman, 2020). Unlike rereading or highlighting, which are often passive forms of studying, active recall forces the brain to work harder, strengthening memory retention and understanding. This active process enables one to analyze, synthesize, and evaluate information better.

Active recall offers significant benefits, particularly in enhancing memory retention and deepening understanding. By actively retrieving information, you strengthen neural pathways, improving long-term recall and identifying gaps in your knowledge. This process fosters a deeper comprehension of material, boosts confidence, and promotes critical thinking by challenging the brain to think through answers rather than merely recognizing them. Additionally, active recall is highly time-efficient, making it a powerful tool for learning complex subjects or preparing for high-stakes situations. Its focus on active engagement ensures that individuals not only retain information but also develop the ability to apply it effectively.

Let us look at one instance of active recall in practice:

Consider learning about the causes of World War II. Instead of rereading a textbook, one might:

1. Write down everything you remember about the topic from memory.

2. Answer practice questions like, what were the economic factors leading to the war?" or How did the Treaty of Versailles contribute?

3. After attempting answers, compare responses with the reference material to identify and address gaps in knowledge.

Other ways to strengthen active recall are to use flashcards while learning, teach or explain the subject to a friend who knows nothing about it, summarize what you read, solve old question papers, or test yourself before an exam (*7 Practical Ways to Apply Active Recall,* 2022).

Active recall technique is particularly helpful in situations where mastery and application of knowledge are essential. For exam preparation, active recall helps students retrieve and apply concepts, such as solving problems in math or constructing analytical essays. It is also invaluable in language learning, reinforcing vocabulary and grammar for conversational fluency. Professionals in fields like medicine, law, or engineering can use active recall to retrieve critical information under pressure, while problem-solving tasks benefit from its ability to strengthen foundational knowledge for innovative solutions. Even in interview preparation, actively recalling facts and experiences ensures confidence and clear articulation, making it a versatile and impactful learning method.

Chunking

Chunking is a cognitive strategy that involves breaking down large amounts of information into smaller, more manageable units or "chunks." This method aligns with how our brain processes and stores information, allowing for better comprehension and retention. By grouping related concepts, chunking helps free up working memory, enabling the learner to focus on analyzing and synthesizing information—key components of HOTS. For example, instead of memorizing a long string of numbers like *0842356478*, chunking it into smaller groups like *084-235-6478* makes it easier to recall.

Chunking is particularly useful in studying complex subjects, problem solving, and skill development. For instance, while learning a new language, breaking down grammar rules or vocabulary into thematic categories makes them easier to grasp. In math or programming, chunking allows learners to break complex problems into smaller steps, promoting analytical thinking. Similarly, professionals in fields like project management or medicine can group related tasks or information for efficient planning and execution.

The benefits of chunking are significant. It reduces cognitive overload, making complex material more digestible. When you organize information into meaningful patterns, it improves memory retention and retrieval. Furthermore, chunking encourages deeper understanding, as it helps learners see relationships between ideas, which is essential for critical thinking and creativity. Chunking is a versatile tool that enhances learning efficiency.

In Practice: Leveraging HOTS for Success

So, where does all this leave us in Tara's case? Can she use HOTS to improve her situation the next time something similar happens? It turns out the answer is a resounding "yes."

1. **Step back and brainstorm:** Before jumping into execution, Tara gathers her team for a brainstorming session to define the campaign's goals, explore creative angles, and identify potential challenges. This would engage the team's collective creativity and ensure alignment from the start.

2. **Apply six thinking hats:** To structure the team's approach, Tara uses the Six Thinking Hats framework to view the project from multiple perspectives. For instance:

   - **White hat:** gather factual data about the client and target audience

   - **Green hat:** encourage creative ideas for innovative marketing

   - **Black hat:** anticipate risks and obstacles

3. **Visualize with mind mapping:** Tara creates a mind map of the campaign, breaking down tasks into categories such as creative design, client communication, and logistical planning. Assigning roles based on expertise clarifies responsibilities and prevents duplication.

4. **Enhance retention and follow-up with spaced repetition:** To address the recurring miscommunications, Tara utilizes spaced repetition to reinforce key project objectives and expectations with her team in follow-up meetings.

As is evident, transitioning to HOTS can increase your productivity, creativity, and even your confidence.

In the next chapter, we shall address one of the most important elements of creative and critical thinking —the power of questioning and how to leverage it.

Key Takeaways

- **HOTS:** HOTS involve critical, creative, and evaluative thinking, enabling problem solving, decision making, and innovation.

- **Brainstorming:** A collaborative process that generates diverse ideas by prioritizing creativity and deferring judgment.

- **Six thinking hats:** A structured thinking method that explores problems from six perspectives (facts, emotions, risks, benefits, creativity, and process) for balanced decision making.

- **Design thinking:** A user-centered approach to problem solving focused on empathy, defining problems, ideating, prototyping, and testing for innovative solutions.

- **Mind mapping:** A visual tool to organize and connect ideas around a central theme, promoting clarity and creative thinking.

- **Spaced repetition:** A learning technique that reinforces knowledge by revisiting material at increasing intervals for better retention.

- **Active recall:** A study method that strengthens memory by actively retrieving information rather than passively reviewing it.

- **Chunking:** A cognitive strategy that breaks information into smaller, manageable units to improve understanding and memory.

Action Steps

1. How can I think critically and creatively in challenging situations?

2. When was the last time I collaborated with others to generate ideas without judgment?

3. Do I consider problems from multiple perspectives, such as emotions, risks, and opportunities?

4. How effectively do I organize my thoughts and ideas visually?

5. Do I iterate and test solutions enough before finalizing them, or do I rush into decisions?

6. How can I practice retrieving information to strengthen my memory and understanding?

7. Do I break down large tasks or information into smaller, digestible parts to make them more manageable?

Chapter 11:

Ask Better, Think Deeper—Increasing Your Level of Questioning

There are no right answers to wrong questions. – Ursula K. Le Guin

Mike is a project manager in a tech company. During a meeting with a potential client, the client outlines their requirements for a new software tool. Mike assumes he understands their needs but does not ask detailed follow-up questions to clarify the specifics, such as: What features are critical vs. optional? What is the client's timeline and budget? Are there any existing systems the tool must integrate with?

Mike is eager to move forward and promises the team will deliver in three months. When development begins, Mike's team discovers they lack clarity on key features. This results in back-and-forth with the client, delaying the project. The client grows frustrated with the delays and perceived lack of professionalism, potentially harming the company's reputation. The team feels overwhelmed by shifting expectations and blames Mike for the lack of upfront clarity, eroding trust within the team.

The pressure to fix the project's issues leads to long hours, affecting his work-life balance. Mike's partner notices his irritability and disengagement at home, leading to arguments and emotional distance. Mike also begins to question his competence, affecting his confidence and motivation.

As you may have guessed, by not asking the right questions, Mike not only jeopardized the project but also created negative ripple effects that strained his professional relationships, team dynamics, and even personal well-being. The importance of curiosity and thoroughness in ensuring clear communication and setting realistic expectations can, therefore, not be emphasized enough.

In this chapter, we shall explore the art of questioning, why it is essential, and how to do it.

The Ins and Outs of Questioning

Good questioning is the heart of critical thinking. It is more than simply asking for information; it is about exploring ideas, busting assumptions, and establishing deeper understanding. High-quality questions push beyond surface-level recall of facts and invite analysis, synthesis, and evaluation. Let us explore what constitutes effective questioning, why it is essential, and how to use questioning strategies to solve problems and inspire innovation.

What Does Good Questioning Look Like?

Effective questions are grounded in Bloom's Taxonomy, particularly its upper levels: Analyze, Evaluate, and Create. These questions go beyond asking for rote answers and instead require participants to think critically and creatively. Let's explore the key characteristics of good questions:

- **Require justification or evidence:** A strong question asks not just for an answer but for the reasoning behind it. For example, instead of asking, "Which is the capital of France?" if you were to ask, "Why do you think Paris became the political and cultural capital of France?" it encourages individuals to think about causation, historical context, or broader implications.

- **Promote comparisons or contrasts:** Questions that ask for comparisons or contrasts force individuals to evaluate similarities, differences, and underlying reasons. For instance, "How does renewable energy compare to fossil fuels in terms of environmental impact and economic feasibility?" fosters a multi-faceted analysis.

- **Encourage the application of concepts:** Effective questions push you to apply your knowledge to real-world scenarios. For example, "How would you apply Newton's laws of motion to design a safer car?" encourages practical thinking and problem solving.

- **Stimulate original ideas:** Creativity is spurred by questions that require unique solutions or perspectives. For example, "What innovative ways could we reduce waste in urban environments?" opens the door to brainstorming and novel solutions.

- **Challenge assumptions:** Queries that question assumptions encourage deeper reflection. For instance, questions like "What if the premise of your argument is flawed? How would that change your conclusion?," compel individuals to evaluate the strength of their reasoning.

Why Is High-Level Questioning Essential?

High-level questioning bolsters critical thinking. Let's examine its benefits:

- **Encourages critical analysis:** High-level questions drive deeper analysis of complex issues by prompting individuals to evaluate evidence, question assumptions, and weigh alternatives.

- **Promotes deeper understanding:** These questions require individuals to synthesize information, draw connections, and articulate nuanced insights, leading to a more comprehensive grasp of the topic.

- **Fosters problem-solving skills:** Good questioning trains individuals to identify problems, explore potential solutions, and justify their choices. For instance, asking, "What strategies could address global food insecurity?" encourages exploration of actionable solutions.

- **Encourages open-mindedness:** Questions that explore different perspectives and challenge preconceived notions foster a mindset of curiosity and openness to alternative viewpoints.

- **Builds transferable skills:** The ability to analyze, evaluate, and create is not confined to a single discipline. These skills are invaluable across professions and everyday life.

- **Stimulates creativity and innovation:** High-level questioning often leads to novel ideas by challenging individuals to think beyond conventional boundaries.

- **Promotes lifelong learning:** Questions that require continuous inquiry and exploration cultivate a habit of learning that lasts a lifetime.

Next, we shall explore some ways in which you can build your questioning skills, one step at a time.

Baseline Questioning: Setting the Foundation

Baseline questions establish a shared understanding and uncover assumptions. These foundational questions are crucial for critical thinking as they:

- **Set a standard:** Baseline questioning helps determine a person's typical demeanor and responses when telling the truth. This is especially useful in interviews or assessments where later questions may probe more sensitive areas.

- **Clarify assumptions:** They reveal underlying assumptions that may influence conclusions. For example, asking, "What do we mean by success in this context?" ensures that everyone operates from a shared definition of the word.

- **Act as a springboard:** Once the basics are clear, these next set of questions pave the way for more complex analysis. For instance, after establishing what the current unemployment rate is, one might ask, "Why is unemployment higher in certain demographics?"

- **Keep discussions focused:** Baseline questions help maintain focus by anchoring the discussion in fundamental facts and definitions, preventing unnecessary tangents.

- **Stimulate engagement:** Starting with accessible questions builds confidence and encourages participants to engage more deeply as the discussion progresses.

Let us now move to questioning with regard to Bloom's Taxonomy.

Bloom's Model for Questioning

Bloom's Taxonomy provides a structured approach to questioning. It distinguishes between lower and higher levels of thinking:

Lower Levels of Thinking

- **Remembering**: recall facts and basic concepts (e.g., "What is the formula for water?")

- **Understanding**: explain ideas or concepts (e.g., "What does the formula for water represent?")

- **Applying**: use information in new situations (e.g., "How would you demonstrate the properties of water in an experiment?")

Higher Levels of Thinking

- **Analyzing**: break down information and explore relationships (e.g., "How do water's properties make it essential for life?")

- **Evaluating**: make judgments and justify decisions (e.g., "Why is water conservation more critical in arid regions?")

- **Creating**: combine information to generate new ideas (e.g., "Design a system to optimize water usage in agriculture.")

Using the above structure, you can craft questions for your specific situation using a lower to higher order of thinking. While lower-order questions will set the base and clarify the fundamentals, higher-order questions will enable nuanced discussion analysis and evaluation, and finally, create unique solutions.

Finally, let us look at Socratic questioning, the pillar of critical thinking.

Socratic Questioning: Questioning the Question

Socratic questioning is a method of disciplined inquiry that challenges assumptions and deepens understanding. It earned its name from the ancient Greek philosopher Socrates, who was known for using a method of inquiry to stimulate critical thinking and illuminate ideas. Socrates would engage his students and interlocutors in dialogue, asking probing questions to challenge assumptions, clarify concepts, and expose contradictions in their thoughts. This method was not about providing answers but guiding others to discover answers for themselves through reflective thinking. The method involves:

- **Clarification questions**: help clarify thoughts or concepts

    - Example: "What do you mean by that?"

- **Probing assumptions**: challenge the basis of beliefs

    - Example: "What are you assuming here?"

- **Evidence and reasons**: explore the foundation of arguments

    - Example: "What evidence supports this view?"

- **Alternative perspectives**: consider other viewpoints

    - Example: "What could someone with a different perspective say about this?"

- **Implications and consequences**: examine the outcomes of ideas

    - Example: "If this is true, what might follow?"

- **Self-reflection**: encourage introspection and self-awareness

    - Example: "Why does this matter to you?"

Socratic questioning adds depth to discussions, moving conversations from surface-level exchanges to meaningful explorations. This method encourages critical thinking, enhances problem-solving skills, and fosters intellectual humility by highlighting the complexity of issues and the limits of one's knowledge.

In Practice: Applying Questioning

Recall the scenario of Mike, the project manager who failed to ask the right questions during a client meeting. Here's how he can use effective questioning strategies to avoid problems later:

1. **Baseline questions**: Mike can ask foundational questions like, "What is the primary goal of this project?" and "What constraints should we consider?" to establish a clear understanding of the project.

2. **Application questions**: To explore the practical implications, Mike might ask, "How do you envision this tool integrating with your existing systems?"

3. **Analysis questions**: Breaking down the client's needs, Mike should ask, "What are the key features you prioritize, and why?"

4. **Evaluation questions**: To assess feasibility, he needs to ask, "How do you foresee this timeline impacting your operations?"

5. **Socratic questions**: To challenge assumptions, Mike should ask, "What are the risks if this project doesn't meet your expectations?" or "What assumptions are we making about the user's needs?"

In asking the above questions, Mike can ensure clarity, alignment, and a stronger relationship with the client. His team will benefit from well-defined objectives, reducing stress and improving outcomes.

Effective questioning is a cornerstone of critical thinking. From establishing baseline understanding to encouraging deep analysis, questions are powerful tools for uncovering insights, solving problems, and fostering creativity. In mastering the art of questioning, individuals can engage more meaningfully with information, develop innovative solutions, and make informed decisions. Whether in professional or personal contexts, the ability to ask good questions is a skill that drives success and cultivates lifelong learning.

In the next chapter, we look at systematized ways of problem solving and go-to methods that will work in most challenges that you are bound to encounter.

Key Takeaways

- **High-level questions**, as opposed to **low-level**, forces us to understand, analyze, evaluate, and create various solutions to the problems at hand.

- **The higher levels of Bloom's Taxonomy** promote questions in line with higher-order thinking.

- **Socratic questioning** entails the questions we ask of ourselves and of others. This contradictory process helps uncover hidden assumptions, biases, and agendas and uncovers clarity in our thinking.

Action Steps

1. When in a quandary, do I ask questions like, "Can you elaborate on that?"

2. Do I frequently ask myself, "Why do I believe this? What evidence supports it?"

3. When seeking solutions, have I asked myself, "Are there other ways to view this situation?"

4. Do I set aside time to reflect on my decisions by asking, "What were my assumptions? Did I examine all the consequences?"

Chapter 12:

Think in the Pause—Mastering Rational Responses for Systemized Planning

Execution is a systematic process of rigorously discussing hows and whats, tenaciously following through, and ensuring accountability. –Lawrence Bossidy

Tallulah, a talented graphic designer often struggles with organization and planning. Her manager assigns her a high-stakes project with a tight deadline: designing a logo for a prestigious client. As she starts, she remembers an offhand comment a colleague made about her ability to meet deadlines. It was true that she sometimes got carried away by the creative process and took slightly longer to accomplish her tasks. Now, the remark stirs insecurities about her past struggles with time management, leaving her feeling defensive and anxious about the present project.

Instead of systematically addressing the project, Tallulah reacts emotionally and dives straight into designing, bypassing essential steps like understanding the client's brief and clarifying project goals. She avoids asking for help or seeking feedback, fearing judgment.

Tallulah finishes the design late because she spends too much time revising details instead of prioritizing critical elements. The client rejects her work, stating it doesn't align with their vision—something she should have clarified upfront. Her team grows frustrated because her lack of communication delays their tasks, affecting the project's overall success.

Sometimes, we become Tallulahs in our lives too. While we know we ought to sort out a problem methodically, we hurriedly jump into it to complete it.

In this chapter, we briefly analyze emotional triggers that often get in the way of thinking critically, as well as measures to stay on top of our work systematically. Understanding triggers and having a plan of action can help us stay motivated and focused on solving and creating.

Emotional Triggers and Coping With Them

A trigger is any person, place, object, or situation that provokes an intense or unexpected emotional reaction or brings up past trauma. Triggers can arise from any sensory input and differ from actual threats, as they involve a non-threatening stimulus activating the body's fight-or-flight response (Cooks-Campbell, 2023).

Triggers could be formed as a result of:

- **Past trauma:** Situations or events that remind someone of traumatic experiences, such as abuse, accidents, or loss.

- **Change:** Major life transitions, whether positive or negative, like a new job or moving, may spark excitement, anxiety, or stress.

- **Negative memories:** Moments tied to failure, embarrassment, or disappointment that evoke similar intense emotions when recalled.

- **Fear:** Phobias and fears, like a fear of heights, can lead to anxiety or panic in related situations.

- **Stressful situations:** High-pressure situations, such as tight deadlines or public speaking, often trigger stress or anxiety.

- **Relationship issues:** Interactions or reminders of past relational conflicts can elicit emotions like sadness, anger, or frustration.

- **Loss or grief:** Anniversaries or events tied to a loss, such as the passing of a loved one, can reignite feelings of sorrow.

Triggers usually start with an experience, when an emotionally intense event occurs, whether traumatic or joyful. Next, we tend to associate certain stimuli, such as sounds or smells, unconsciously to the emotional experience. The brain stores these associations, as memories, enabling stimuli to evoke strong emotions long after the event. When encountering similar stimuli later, the brain is triggered and we react as though reliving the original event, even without a conscious awareness of the connection. When triggered, individuals may feel anxious, cry, panic, withdraw, act out, or become defensive.

Coping with emotional triggers requires both critical thinking and intentional action. Here's a structured approach to understanding and dealing with emotional triggers while maintaining personal and professional growth:

- **Understand your emotional landscape:** Critical thinking begins with self-awareness. Take the time to recognize and analyze your emotional patterns. When you feel triggered, pause to ask yourself: *What am I feeling, and why? What specific situations or interactions tend to provoke these emotions?* You can identify the root causes of your triggers by journaling or reflecting on recurring patterns. This allows you to anticipate and prepare for challenging situations in both personal and professional contexts.

- **Pause and respond thoughtfully:** When triggered, resist the urge to react immediately. Instead, step back and apply critical thinking to assess the situation. Consider: *What exactly about this situation is causing this reaction? Is my response proportional or based on past experiences?* Taking a break from the immediate environment provides space to process emotions. At work, use tools like rephrasing questions or asking for clarification to buy time and compose your thoughts. This helps maintain professionalism while managing emotional intensity.

- **Establish mindfulness and grounding routines:** Meditation, deep breathing, or progressive muscle relaxation can help you remain present and observe your emotions without judgment. Structured routines or grounding techniques can help you manage stress in the moment. For example, if a triggering event occurs during a meeting, practice controlled breathing to calm your mind and stay engaged.

- **Recognize physical reactions:** Triggers often manifest as physical sensations—a racing heart, clenched jaw, or tight chest. Memorizing these physical cues empowers you to transition from reaction mode to a more intentional, proactive state of mind.

- **Prioritize self-care:** Personal well-being directly influences professional performance. Emotional triggers can be exhausting, so maintaining physical and emotional health is crucial. Ensure you're addressing basic needs like sleep, nutrition, and hydration. Incorporate regular self-care practices into your routine to bolster your resilience against stressors, whether they arise at home or at work.

- **Set healthy boundaries:** Clearly defined and communicated boundaries reduce the likelihood of encountering triggering situations. For example, in personal relationships, communicate your emotional needs and limits. In professional settings, manage expectations by being clear about your workload and deadlines. Being assertive in setting boundaries helps protect your emotional energy and maintain focus on your goals.

- **Build a support network:** A strong support system—whether friends, family, colleagues, or professional groups—is invaluable. Sharing your experiences with trusted individuals can provide fresh perspectives and emotional validation. In the workplace, finding allies or mentors who understand your challenges can foster a more supportive and empathetic environment.

- **Integrate personal growth with professional goals:** Managing emotional triggers is also about aligning your personal development with your professional aspirations. Use critical thinking to identify how unresolved emotional patterns might impact your career and relationships. Next, set actionable goals for personal growth, such as improving communication skills or enhancing EI. Apply these skills to build stronger professional relationships and navigate workplace dynamics more effectively.

- **Seek professional support:** Some triggers are deeply rooted and require expert guidance to address them effectively. A therapist, counselor, or coach can help you with specialized techniques such as cognitive behavioral therapy (CBT), EMDR, or exposure therapy. In professional contexts, seeking mentorship or coaching can provide additional tools to manage work-related stressors and triggers.

Coping with emotional triggers requires blending critical thinking, emotional awareness, and intentional action. This holistic approach ensures that you're managing emotional responses and cultivating resilience and clarity in both your personal and professional life. Since growth takes time, it's essential to celebrate small victories as you work toward greater emotional and professional balance.

In light of emotional triggers and anxiety, we shall now look at how to work on problems and get work done.

Systematized Problem Solving

Systematic problem solving is a methodical approach to the questions you have, coming up with the best plan of action and executing it. However, it doesn't just end there. It also involves a series of revisits to the issue to understand what can be streamlined and improved further so that your work becomes that much easier the next time around (*What is* Problem-Solving?, 2024; *8-Step Problem-Solving Process,* n.d.). The steps to this are:

1. **Define the problem:** Clearly articulate the issue at hand. Is it a recurring emotional trigger, a challenging work dynamic, or a specific situation? Being precise about the problem ensures a focused approach to finding solutions.

2. **Clarify the problem:** Dig deeper into the problem to understand its nuances. Ask critical questions to identify the specific circumstances or behaviors contributing to the issue. This step helps avoid misdiagnosing the problem.

3. **Define goals:** Determine what success looks like. What are you trying to achieve? For example, do you want to reduce stress at work or manage emotional triggers more effectively? Setting clear goals provides direction.

4. **Identify root causes:** Analyze the underlying reasons for the problem. Use tools like the "5 Whys" or root cause analysis to uncover contributing factors. Understanding the root causes ensures solutions address the core issue, not just the symptoms.

5. **Develop an action plan:** Brainstorm and evaluate feasible solutions. Choose actions that align with your goals and are realistic within your personal or professional constraints. Break the plan into manageable steps to ensure consistent progress.

6. **Execute the action plan:** Implement the chosen solutions methodically. Stay committed and monitor your progress regularly. Address any obstacles that arise during execution to maintain momentum.

7. **Evaluate results:** Review the outcomes of your action plan. Did it resolve the problem or improve the situation? Use metrics or feedback to assess whether your goals were achieved.

8. **Identify alternatives:** If the initial plan didn't fully address the problem, consider alternative solutions. Learn from what didn't work and adapt your approach to achieve better results.

9. **Continuously improve:** Embrace a growth mindset. Regularly evaluate your strategies and refine them over time. In both personal and professional contexts, continuous improvement ensures long-term resilience and success.

Solving problems effectively involves a clear and structured approach. This step-by-step method not only resolves challenges but also boosts confidence and adaptability in tackling future obstacles.

In Practice

Briefly going back to Tallulah's problem we realize the issue lies in her reactive and unsystematic approach to problem solving, compounded by her emotional trigger—her colleague's comment. Her emotional reaction caused her to rush into tasks without clarity, leading to professional and personal consequences.

She can easily handle a similar situation in the future better if:

- she acknowledges her emotional reaction and uses it as an opportunity for self-reflection, asking herself, *Why does this comment bother me? Is it factual, or just my fear speaking? Is there a history to it?*

    - **Tip**: Take a moment to breathe, calm down, and focus on the task instead of reacting emotionally.

- before diving into design, she can systematically gather all the necessary information, ask questions to understand the client's needs and create a clear plan.

    - **Tip**: Create a checklist: Do I fully understand the plan? Are there areas I need to clarify?

- she breaks the project into smaller tasks with deadlines for each step, ensuring progress and focus.

    - **Action**: Use a project management tool or a simple to-do list to structure her tasks by priority.

- she openly communicates with her team and manager, ensuring her work meets expectations and reducing the pressure she feels.

    - **Action**: Schedule regular check-ins with yourself, and others to share updates and receive feedback.

A change in attitude would greatly benefit Tallulah in working on her problem-solving skills.

(Re-)Learning to Look at Problems as Creative Opportunities Rather Than as Obstacles

Adam Grant explores the concept of creative or productive procrastination in his book *Originals: How Non-Conformists Move the World* (2016). He argues that procrastination, when used strategically, can be a powerful tool for enhancing creativity and generating original ideas. Rather than viewing procrastination as purely negative, he distinguishes between passive procrastination, which is avoidance that leads to stress and inefficiency, and productive procrastination, or the deliberate delay in working on problems that allows ideas to incubate.

Grant highlights that taking time to delay a task allows the mind to wander and explore unconventional ideas. This period of incubation promotes creativity by enabling a broader exploration of possibilities. For instance, famous figures like Leonardo da Vinci and Martin Luther King Jr. used procrastination to refine their groundbreaking ideas and approaches.

However, extreme procrastination can lead to missed deadlines and poor-quality work, but moderate procrastination can create space for innovation. Grant uses research to show that individuals who procrastinate moderately tend to produce more creative solutions than "precrastinators"—those who rush to finish early, or chronic procrastinators—who wait until the last minute.

To make procrastination productive, Grant suggests working on lower-priority tasks or brainstorming ideas while delaying the primary task. This keeps the mind engaged and fosters creative insights.

Ultimately, successful individuals, especially entrepreneurs and professionals with a positive mindset, view problems as opportunities for growth, learning, and improvement (DeMers, 2015). This perspective reduces stress, contextualizes challenges, promotes adaptability, and builds resilience over time. While there's no quick fix to develop this mindset, it's achievable through consistent effort. Some steps you could work on include the following:

1. **Accept that problems are natural:** Recognize that problems, big and small, are a normal and inevitable part of life.

2. **Neutralize first impressions:** Avoid forming negative judgments by stating the problem objectively rather than as a nuisance or trouble for you.

3. **Distance yourself:** Detach yourself emotionally and describe the problem as if it were happening to someone else.

4. **Evaluate threats and consequences objectively:** Calmly distinguish real consequences from exaggerated fears to avoid overreacting.

5. **Focus on improvements instead of reactions:** Reframe problems as opportunities to make adjustments or take preventative measures.

In the next chapter, we look at two tools that could further help us create innovatively without compromising on our strategic thinking skills.

Key Takeaways

- **Identifying triggers and emotional awareness**: Learn to identify triggers and address them constructively rather than letting them control your actions.

- **Systematic planning**: Establish a step-by-step approach to tasks, ensuring clarity and prioritization.

- **Looking at problems as opportunities rather than obstacles** will realign your mindset to a more positive one as you work on troubleshooting.

- **Productive procrastination** is playing around with a problem and exploring it from all possible angles instead of jumping in with mediocre solutions just to get the problem out of the way.

Action Steps

1. How do I usually respond to emotional triggers—does this response serve my long-term well-being?

2. Think of a particular setback you are facing now. How can this setback teach me something valuable or push me toward personal growth that I wouldn't have pursued otherwise?

3. If I were to view this situation as a chance to grow stronger or more resilient, what specific action could I take today?

Chapter 13:

AI and Us—Critical Thinking in the Age of LLMs

...hallucination is all LLMs do. They are dream machines. We direct their dreams with prompts... —Andrej Karpathy

Rachel is a software developer tasked with building a feature for her company's website: an automated email system that personalizes reminders based on user activity. She's excited about the project but knows it involves writing a complex algorithm to parse user data, set conditions, and trigger appropriate responses—a task that could take days or even weeks if done manually.

Instead of starting from scratch, Rachel decides to use an AI coding assistant. She starts by describing the task in detail:

"Write a Python script that checks user activity logs, identifies inactive users for 30 days, and sends them a personalized reminder email. It should connect to an SMTP server for email delivery."

The AI quickly generates a code template. However, Rachel doesn't stop there. She carefully reviews the output, spotting an issue where the script isn't handling edge cases like invalid email addresses. She refines her prompts:

"Add functionality to validate email addresses before sending reminders. If an email is invalid, log it separately with an error message."

With this improved input, the AI refines the code, and Rachel runs a test. She identifies another gap: the system lacks a retry mechanism for failed emails. Rachel adjusts her query again:

"Add logic to retry sending emails up to three times if the initial attempt fails due to server issues."

Through this iterative process, Rachel creates a fully functional, efficient script in just a few hours. Had she attempted to write the entire code manually, she would've spent days researching Simple Mail Transfer Protocols (SMTP), debugging syntax errors, and optimizing logic.

Although the AI expedited Rachel's work, her success was tied to her ability to ask the right questions. Without well-thought-out prompts, the AI's initial outputs might have been insufficient or incorrect. Rachel's expertise, creativity, and problem-solving skills ensured the AI provided relevant and accurate solutions.

Rachel's experience highlights a broader truth: much like coding with AI, navigating life challenges often hinges on asking the right questions. When we articulate our needs and goals clearly—whether to ourselves or an AI—we unlock pathways to faster, better solutions. In this chapter, we shall look at unlocking the powers of Large Language Models (LLMs) and AI technology to improve our critical thinking and get work done smarter and faster.

Using LLMs to Enhance Critical Thinking: How AI Can Stimulate Deeper Thought

In an age dominated by digital innovation, LLMs like ChatGPT and other chatbots are becoming indispensable tools for individuals looking to elevate their cognitive abilities. These advanced AI systems go beyond simple assistance; they actively foster critical thinking by serving as collaborators that stimulate deeper thought, broaden perspectives, and encourage analytical skills. We can take significant strides in enhancing our cognitive processes, leveraging their capabilities. Here is how LLMs contribute to building critical thinking.

LLMs as Catalysts for Cognitive Exploration

At their core, LLMs act as catalysts, sparking cognitive exploration. They enable users to go beyond surface-level understanding by providing insights that encourage the exploration of nuanced ideas. For instance, when presented with an open-ended question, an LLM doesn't merely offer a single response. Instead, it generates a range of ideas, interpretations, and pathways for further inquiry, prompting users to think more expansively.

This facilitation of intellectual curiosity positions LLMs as powerful companions for anyone seeking to analyze or dissect complex topics. Guiding users through structured thought processes and presenting unexpected angles, LLMs enable the creation of richer, more well-rounded solutions and conclusions.

Enhanced Introspection

Critical thinking often starts with self-reflection. LLMs can boost introspection by prompting users to evaluate their beliefs, assumptions, and biases. For example, when someone inputs a personal perspective or argument, an LLM can pose follow-up questions that challenge the validity or completeness of that viewpoint. This ability to act as a reflective sounding board encourages users to dig deeper into their own reasoning processes.

Furthermore, LLMs can help clarify thoughts by translating abstract ideas into structured language. This makes it easier to identify gaps in reasoning and refine conclusions. Users can actively engage with LLMs by crafting prompts that challenge their existing beliefs or seek alternative explanations. For instance, asking, "What are potential blind spots in my argument?" or "How might someone with a different perspective view this issue?" can yield thought-provoking insights. Engaging in iterative dialogue, where each response prompts deeper questioning, allows individuals to refine their reasoning and achieve greater clarity in their thought processes.

Combining LLMs into Our Thought Process

The integration of LLMs into our cognitive workflow represents a shift in how we approach problems, ideate, and make decisions. Acting as thought partners, LLMs can:

- provide quick access to varied perspectives.

- help structure ideas systematically.

- prompt users to question their assumptions.

In other words, it can play pivotal roles in various real-world scenarios, such as assisting professionals in brainstorming innovative solutions to complex business challenges, helping students break down dense academic material into manageable concepts, or enabling writers to refine their ideas for clearer communication. They provide quick access to diverse perspectives, help structure ideas systematically for actionable outcomes, and prompt users to question their assumptions, fostering a mindset of continuous learning and critical analysis.

This symbiotic relationship doesn't replace human cognition but augments it. The effectiveness of this partnership, however, depends on the quality of the prompts we provide. Just as asking the right questions is essential in life, formulating clear and precise queries is key to unlocking the full potential of LLMs. The result is a seamless integration of human creativity and machine efficiency.

LLMs and the Cognitive Journey

LLMs enhance our cognitive journey, serving as both guides and co-travelers in the pursuit of knowledge. Their ability to process vast amounts of information quickly and present it in an accessible format makes them invaluable tools for intellectual exploration. Here are specific ways they aid critical thinking:

- **Facilitating inquiry and exploration:** LLMs respond to open-ended questions, refine them, and suggest follow-ups. For example, if you ask about the impacts of climate change, an LLM might provide an overview and then propose related questions like, "How does deforestation contribute to climate change?" or "What are the economic implications of renewable energy adoption?" This dynamic interaction encourages users to ask clarifying or probing questions, deepening their analysis of the subject matter.

- **Encouraging multiple perspectives:** LLMs can present alternative viewpoints or challenge biases by simulating different perspectives. For instance, in a debate about universal healthcare, an LLM might outline both the benefits (e.g., increased accessibility) and the drawbacks (e.g., potential strain on resources). Exposing users to diverse viewpoints, LLMs foster open-mindedness and the ability to critically evaluate conflicting ideas.

- **Simplifying complex topics:** LLMs can break down intricate ideas into smaller, more digestible parts. For example, they can explain quantum mechanics in layman's terms before diving into more advanced concepts. Simplifying complexity ensures clarity at the baseline level, which is crucial for higher-order critical thinking.

- **Encouraging creative problem solving:** LLMs can suggest hypothetical scenarios, ask "what-if" questions, or brainstorm solutions. For example, in response to a challenge of reducing urban pollution, an LLM might propose innovative ideas like vertical gardens, improved public transit systems, or smart traffic management. This stimulates innovative and evaluative thinking, encouraging users to approach problems from unconventional angles.

- **Assisting in structuring arguments:** AI can help outline and organize arguments or counterarguments for essays, debates, or discussions. For instance, when tasked with writing about the ethical implications of AI, an LLM can suggest sections such as "Benefits of AI," "Potential Risks," and "Ethical Guidelines." Structuring arguments logically is a cornerstone of critical reasoning, and LLMs make this process more intuitive.

- **Acting as a Socratic questioner:** LLMs can emulate the Socratic Method by asking thought-provoking questions. For example, if you assert that renewable energy is the ultimate solution to climate change, an LLM might ask, "What challenges might arise in implementing renewable energy globally?" or "Are there situations where non-renewable energy might still be necessary?" This encourages users to justify their assumptions and critically examine their thought processes, honing their reasoning skills.

- **Providing instant feedback:** LLMs can review arguments or analyses and suggest improvements. For instance, they can point out logical inconsistencies, highlight missing evidence, or propose alternative interpretations. Benefit: Instant feedback helps refine critical thinking by identifying gaps and strengthening reasoning.

- **Enhancing access to diverse resources:** LLMs can summarize, compare, and explain content from various fields. For example, they can integrate insights from psychology, history, and economics to provide a multidisciplinary perspective on a topic like leadership. In synthesizing ideas across domains, LLMs promote a holistic approach to critical thinking.

The integration of LLMs into our intellectual toolkit hints at a huge change in how we approach problems, ideate, and make decisions. These models encourage a shift from reactive to proactive thinking by providing a structured framework for exploration. Rather than merely reacting to challenges, users can anticipate and maneuver complexities with confidence.

Changes in Problem Solving and Decision Making

Google and other tech giants are working on LLMs emerging as transformative tools for small businesses. Such apps allow users to easily manage tasks like analyzing job applications, evaluating financial data, and identifying trends (Marks, 2024). There is even a new update facilitating an interactive mode for audio podcasts, featuring lifelike AI-generated hosts capable of real-time dialogue with users (Werner, 2024). This technology will enable users to actively participate in the podcast experience, pose questions, provide comments, and receive contextual responses. The AI hosts display natural human-like voice inflections, timing, and tone, creating an immersive and engaging conversational environment. The natural conversational interface makes it accessible to individuals of all technical skill levels, fostering a seamless user experience. Moreover, the AI's dynamic and tailored responses make it ideal for tutoring, mentoring, or brainstorming.

AI transformation, like the above, extends to decision-making processes as well. LLMs help users weigh options more carefully and consider long-term implications, presenting data-driven insights and challenging assumptions. The result is a more deliberate and informed approach to problem solving.

The advent of LLMs represents a significant leap forward in enhancing critical thinking. However, the effectiveness of this partnership ultimately depends on our ability to engage thoughtfully with the technology. Using LLMs effectively requires clarity, precision, and intentionality. When harnessed correctly, they do not merely provide answers but inspire deeper thought, broaden horizons, and equip us with the tools to navigate an increasingly complex world. As we continue to integrate AI into our lives, the fusion of human ingenuity and machine intelligence promises a future where critical thinking flourishes like never before.

Key Takeaways

LLMs backed by **AI technology** are advanced artificial intelligence systems designed to process, analyze, and generate human-like text, enabling meaningful interactions that support learning, creativity, and problem solving. LLMs can:

- provide fast access to various perspectives and different subjects.
- help organize ideas methodically.
- help users ask questions and question their own biases.

Action Steps

1. How do I currently engage with AI tools, and what opportunities am I missing to enhance my learning or productivity?

2. In what ways could incorporating LLMs into my thought process improve my problem solving or decision-making skills?

3. What are some potential risks or biases of relying on AI for insights, and how can I mitigate them while using LLMs effectively?

4. How can I balance the use of AI with my own intuition and
    reasoning to ensure I maintain a human-centric approach to
    decision making?

Chapter 14:

Positive Pathways—Optimistic Decision Making

You may not control all the events that happen to you, but you can decide not to be reduced by them. —Maya Angelou

Nina, a teacher, wakes up to find an urgent email from her principal asking for a revised presentation of an event to be delivered by noon. Initially, Nina felt overwhelmed by the tight deadline and the amount of work needed to make changes. This crossroads of thought triggers two possible paths in how Nina approaches the situation.

Path 1—The Negative Spiral: Nina fixates on the lack of time and blames the principal for not providing clear guidance earlier. *Why does this always happen to me?* they think, frustration mounting. As they work, they constantly criticize themselves for not preparing a better draft beforehand. This mindset leads to stress, mistakes in the presentation, and a rushed delivery that doesn't resonate well with the board. By the end of the day, Nina feels drained, defeated, and resentful of both her job and themselves.

Path 2—The Positive Frame: Nina decides to view the challenge as an opportunity to grow and showcase her adaptability. They remind themselves, *I've handled tight deadlines before, and I can do this again.* Nina quickly prioritizes the most impactful changes, takes a short break to clear her mind, and asks for quick feedback from a colleague to ensure the presentation hits the mark. The revised presentation is delivered on time and impresses the board. Nina ends the day feeling accomplished, proud of her problem-solving skills, and optimistic about future challenges.

As is evident, the same situation can lead to vastly different outcomes depending on Nina's decision-making approach and mindset. It isn't rocket science to figure out which of the two paths above one ought to choose.

When you choose positivity and focus on what can be controlled, you can turn a potentially negative day into a productive and fulfilling one.

Viewing decisions through a constructive lens can uplift one's mood, confidence, and overall outlook. Conversely, a negative perspective can cloud judgment, magnify stress, and hinder success. Let us look at what positive decision making is and how one can achieve it.

Positive Decision Making: A Life Skill

Barry Schwartz's TED Talk on "practical wisdom" (2009) highlights the necessity of balancing rules and incentives with human judgment to navigate the complexities of modern life. He argues that while rules provide structure and incentives to motivate human behavior, they are insufficient for addressing nuanced, real-world situations. Practical wisdom, rooted in Aristotle's philosophy, combines moral insight with the skill to act appropriately in varying contexts. Schwartz emphasizes that this form of moral wisdom allows individuals to interpret rules flexibly, exercise empathy, and adapt solutions to fit unique circumstances.

Schwartz critiques the overreliance on bureaucratic systems and rigid regulations, which often strip individuals of their autonomy and ability to make moral decisions aligned with the specific contexts they are placed in. For instance, he talks of the experienced janitor who skips mopping the floor because an elderly patient is walking around getting a little exercise. Schwartz underscores the importance of cultivating practical wisdom in professions like education, healthcare, and law, where human connections and nuanced judgment are critical. Environments that prioritize learning through experience, mentorship, and ethical reasoning are necessary for societies to empower individuals to make better decisions and improve collective well-being. Practical wisdom, Schwartz concludes, is essential for creating a compassionate, effective, and morally grounded society.

If there is one takeaway from Barry Schwartz's talk, then it is the vital need for empathetic and context-sensitive decision making. What this means is being human-centric in our decisions. Let us explore the ins and outs of this.

Positive decision making is more than just a tool for navigating life's challenges; it's a mindset that can shape your experiences, enhance your well-being, and empower you to lead a fulfilling life. This chapter explores the concept of positive decision making as a transferable skill and explores its applications across various domains of life. Along the way, we'll examine obstacles to its transferability and how to overcome them.

The Power of Positive Decision Making

At its core, positive decision making involves making choices that align with your values, foster growth, and enhance your overall quality of life. It is a skill that evolves with practice and reflection, becoming a cornerstone of personal and professional success. What makes it particularly impactful is its adaptability—it can be applied across multiple contexts, making it a versatile and essential skill.

Transferability of Positive Decision Making

One of the most remarkable aspects of positive decision making is its transferability. This means that once you cultivate this skill, you can apply it to different areas of your life with significant benefits. Let's explore its applications in various contexts:

- **Personal life:** Positive decision making helps you navigate relationships, set boundaries, and prioritize self-care effectively. Some examples would include:

  - **Relationships:** Choosing to engage in honest communication and fostering mutual respect strengthens connections with loved ones.

  - **Boundaries:** Learning to say "no" when necessary protects your mental and emotional health.

  - **Self-care:** Deciding to allocate time for rest and activities that rejuvenate you enhances your overall well-being.

- **Professional settings:** In the workplace, positive decision making is vital for sound judgment, teamwork, problem solving, and leadership roles. For instance:

- **Teamwork:** Collaborating effectively by considering others' perspectives creates a harmonious work environment.

- **Problem solving:** Analyzing options and choosing solutions that benefit the team and organization leads to better outcomes.

- **Leadership:** Making ethical and empathetic decisions inspires trust and motivates colleagues.

- **Academic contexts:** For students, positive decision making enhances critical thinking, time management, and the ability to handle stress under pressure. Examples include:

  - **Critical Thinking:** Evaluating evidence and making informed choices improves academic performance.

  - **Time management:** Allocating time to prioritize tasks ensures efficiency and reduces last-minute stress.

  - **Stress management:** Choosing healthy coping mechanisms, like taking breaks or seeking support, fosters resilience during exams and deadlines.

- **Social interactions:** In social settings, positive decision making fosters empathy, conflict resolution, and maintaining healthy friendships. Consider:

  - **Empathy:** Actively listening and responding to others with kindness strengthens relationships.

  - **Conflict resolution:** Approaching disagreements with a mindset of collaboration rather than confrontation reduces tension.

  - **Friendship:** Making consistent, thoughtful choices builds trust and loyalty.

- **Unexpected challenges:** Positive decision making equips you with adaptability and resilience when facing crises or sudden changes. For example:

  - **Adaptability:** Choosing to embrace change and seeking constructive solutions helps you navigate uncertainty.

- o **Resilience:** Focusing on what you can control and maintaining a growth mindset allows you to bounce back from setbacks.

While positive decision making is inherently transferable, several obstacles can hinder its application across different domains.

Obstacles to the Transferability of Positive Decision Making

Understanding barriers to the transferability of positive decision making is the first step toward overcoming them:

- **Context-dependence:** Some decisions may seem specific to a particular scenario, making it challenging to see how the same principles apply elsewhere. Overcoming this requires recognizing underlying patterns and transferable lessons in past decisions and reflecting on how similar values or approaches can guide choices in new contexts.

- **Lack of exposure to diverse scenarios:** Limited life experiences can restrict your ability to apply positive decision making universally. To address this, seek out new experiences and challenges to broaden your perspective. Also, engage in simulations or role-playing exercises to practice decision making in varied situations.

- **Cognitive biases:** Unconscious biases can cloud judgment and limit effective decision making. Therefore, become aware of common biases, such as confirmation bias or overconfidence. Then, actively seek diverse viewpoints to challenge your assumptions.

- **Emotional interference:** Strong emotions can disrupt rational decision making, leading to impulsive choices. You can practice mindfulness to regulate emotions and maintain clarity. Similarly, pause to reflect before making important decisions.

- **Cultural and social norms:** Societal expectations and cultural norms may influence your choices in ways that conflict with positive decision making. To handle this, identify your core values and prioritize them in your decisions. Respect cultural differences while maintaining authenticity in your choices.

- **Knowledge gaps:** A lack of information can hinder your ability to make informed decisions. Continuously seek knowledge and stay curious. Consult trusted sources or experts when faced with uncertainty.

- **Overreliance on technology:** While using technology is good, relying on it to the extent that you forget to make use of your own resources can be negative. Dependence on digital tools can reduce critical thinking and decision making autonomy. Striving to strike a balance between leveraging technology and independent reasoning is vital.

- **Rigid thinking patterns:** Critical thinking goes hand in hand with the agility of thinking because fixed mindsets may limit the ability to adapt to new circumstances. Embracing flexibility and openness to change are essential for growth.

Ultimately, positive decision making is about making choices that are right for you—aligned with your values, goals, and unique circumstances. You can unlock its full potential and use it to navigate life with confidence and purpose by understanding its transferability and addressing potential obstacles.

The "Right-for-You" Approach

As you cultivate positive decision-making skills, remember that it's a journey of growth and adaptation. Each decision you make, big or small, is an opportunity to learn and refine your approach. In doing so, you empower yourself to lead a life filled with positivity, resilience, and success.

There are no universally "right" or "wrong" choices in decision making. The key lies in making decisions "right for you"—those that align with your values, goals, and circumstances. Perhaps it also means moral and practical wisdom which may contravene some of the established rules and regulations too. Such a personalized approach can significantly impact your happiness and mental well-being.

- **Subjective happiness:** A "right" decision is one that brings satisfaction and aligns with your aspirations. Recognizing that happiness is subjective empowers you to prioritize what matters most to you.

- **Learning opportunities:** Even decisions perceived as "wrong" provide valuable lessons. Viewing mistakes as opportunities for growth fosters resilience and adaptability.

- **Mental health awareness:** Avoid overthinking or striving for perfection. Focus on decisions that reduce stress and contribute to your overall fulfillment.

- **Long-term perspective:** Short-term discomfort may lead to long-term happiness and vice versa. Evaluating the broader impact of your choices can help balance immediate and future needs.

- **Self-compassion:** Accept that your decisions may not always please others. Prioritize choices that respect your well-being and align with your authentic self.

Positive decision making is a transformative skill, enabling individuals to embrace a "right for you" mindset. Overcoming barriers, you can harness its power to enhance every aspect of your life. Whether managing personal relationships, advancing professionally, or adapting to unexpected challenges, this skill equips you to thrive in an ever-changing world.

Continuing on the theme of practical wisdom, we shall look at the joys of collaborative decision making in the next chapter.

Key Takeaways

- **Practical wisdom:** Critical thinking is incomplete without contextual, empathetic, and human choices that need not always be bound by rigid rules of action and behavior.

- **Positive decision making:** The ability to view opportunities rather than obstacles in whatever life presents you with—the challenges, too.

1. Am I rigid in accepting and applying rules and regulations even when sticking to them can go against their basic purpose?

2. Do I deliberately embrace experiences and challenges, in particular to broaden my horizon?

3. Do I seek out other opinions to understand biases and prejudices that I may unconsciously carry?

4. Am I too reliant on "right choices" rather than "right-for-me" choices? How do I transition from one to the other?

Chapter 15:

The Power of Perspective—Creative Thinking Through Collective Insights

In a world where you can be anything, be kind. –Anonymous

James, a product manager at a fast-growing tech startup, was known for his decisive nature and innovative ideas. His team was preparing for a critical product launch—a new project management app that could set the company apart from its competitors.

During a brainstorming session, James pitched his vision for the app's design: a bold, flashy interface that he believed would grab users' attention. However, his team—composed of UX designers, developers, and marketers—voiced a different opinion. They emphasized that simplicity and user-friendliness were what customers truly valued based on their research and past feedback.

Initially, James felt hesitant. After all, he was leading the project, and this idea was something he was passionate about. But instead of digging in his heels, he paused and reflected on the collective expertise of his team. He remembered that great leadership meant trusting the people you work with.

James decided to set aside his personal preferences and go with the team's approach. They focused on creating an app that prioritized ease of use, clean design, and intuitive navigation.

When launch day arrived, the results were staggering. Users praised the app's simplicity and functionality, driving record downloads within the first month. Industry reviewers highlighted the team's thoughtful design, and customers shared positive feedback across platforms.

At the celebration dinner, James stood up and raised a toast to the insight and expertise of his colleagues. His decision to embrace his team's wisdom not only resulted in a successful product but strengthened their collaboration and trust for future projects. James realized that sometimes, true leadership lies in stepping back and letting the team shine.

Collaborative Decision Making and Critical Thinking

In a fast-paced world, effective decision making stands as a cornerstone of success. Yet, making the right call isn't always about consensus or unilateral authority. Collaborative decision making, rooted in critical thinking, allows individuals and teams to navigate complexity with agility and foresight. We shall explore the principles of making sound decisions quickly, harnessing the power of collective wisdom, and leveraging teamwork to tackle big problems.

Making Good Decisions, Quickly

In most high-stakes scenarios, time is often limited. Good decision making is about striking a balance between speed and thoroughness. This balance can be achieved by following a few sound steps:

- **Avoid consensus-seeking and unilateral decisions:** Collaborative decision making does not mean everyone has to agree. Instead, it means valuing diverse perspectives and trusting the expertise of those closest to the problem.

- **Seek input from the ground level:** Decision making should involve those with the most hands-on experience, not necessarily those with formal authority. These individuals often have a clearer understanding of the problem's nuances because they are working most closely with the product or idea.

- **Address the root cause:** We know that medicines only go to a certain extent in fixing illnesses. Diseases can be really cured only by addressing the root causes, such as lack of proper physical rest or poor nutrition or exercise. Similarly, effective decisions must tackle the core issue rather than the symptoms. One needs to find out why there are recurring problems and prevent them from happening again. This approach ensures long-term solutions rather than quick fixes.

- **Consider the big picture:** Evaluate the problem holistically, weighing both short-term impacts and long-term consequences, before making choices. Sometimes, short-term benefits will need to be considered over the long-term results, while at other times, this approach will need to be reversed.

- **Assume accountability:** A good decision-maker owns the outcome, whether it succeeds or fails, creating a sense of responsibility. Blaming others or criticizing them without holding yourself accountable will only undermine trust within the team.

- **Communicate decisions clearly:** Stakeholders need time to process and adapt to decisions. Clear communication ensures the alignment of needs and readiness.

- **Build flexibility into decisions:** Make choices with the understanding that they may need to evolve. This adaptability allows for refinement as new information emerges during the process.

Closely aligned to the art of making good decisions quickly, we shall look at what teaming is all about.

The Art of Teaming

Teaming has become essential in today's interconnected, fast-paced work environment. Many types of work today have agile teams, and you may end up working with different people, perhaps even located in different parts of the world, as the work progresses. Such teams on the go often face challenges such as varying time zones, skill sets, cultural differences, and conflicting professional norms. Despite these hurdles, effective teamwork can lead to innovative solutions, especially for complex problems. Remember the Chilean mine disaster we discussed in the Introduction? Despite the rescue operations being conducted by different people across the globe, the mission was a success precisely because the participants were willing to team up and put the problem first.

However, there are a few essential requirements for teaming to be a success (Edmondson, 2018). They are:

Key Values for Successful Teaming

1. **Humility:** Recognize that the problem is bigger than any individual. Thus, letting go of personal competitiveness will build collaboration and collective focus.

2. **Curiosity:** Stay open to new ideas, willing to unlearn and relearn any number of times. This mindset ensures adaptability and growth.

3. **Willingness to take risks:** Embrace uncertainty as an opportunity to learn. Calculated risk-taking is often necessary for groundbreaking solutions. If you only remain cautious, the results will be repetitive and safe, and probably fine too, but never brilliant or break-through.

Harnessing Collective Creativity

Innovation thrives on collective creativity (Hill, 2015). It's a messy, iterative process involving trial and error. Teams can develop solutions that are greater than the sum of their parts by embracing different talents and perspectives. This process involves:

- **Creative abrasion:** Encouraging productive debates and discourse to refine ideas. All may not always be smooth sailing, but there will always be progress and a free flow of ideas, which may spur on more ideas.

- **Creative agility:** Testing and refining ideas through cycles of reflection and adjustment, combining scientific precision with artistic intuition. This means that there may not always be a perfect blueprint in place to start with. There will be several products or ideas created simultaneously that may need to be scrapped, redone, combined, or modified as the need arises.

- **Creative resolution:** Integrating opposing ideas into cohesive solutions, demonstrating the power of synthesis. Understanding that what looks opposing may not always be so, and that different ideas can exist in unison, and be worked into the final product or idea, is at the core of this. In other words, it may be possible to implement Plan A, which seems antithetical to Plan

B, and then later, perhaps also apply Plan B at a different stage of the product or idea.

Empowering those closest to the problem through a bottom-up approach allows for freedom and innovation. This inverted pyramid of authority ensures that the best solutions emerge from collective effort rather than hierarchical mandates from people who aren't working closest to the problem.

Practice in Reverse

Let us consider an alternate scenario of James bypassing his team's advice and moving forward with his design, now. The app would have launched with a flashy interface but quickly encountered user backlash. Reviews might have criticized the app as confusing and impractical, leading to poor adoption rates. The company would face reputational damage and significant financial loss, forcing them to redesign the app post-launch. The setback would delay their market competitiveness and strain team morale. The team would feel disgruntled that James did not listen to them but that they were having to rework everything now against their choice.

By contrast, James's decision to embrace collaborative wisdom in the actual scenario resulted in an app celebrated for its simplicity and functionality. The team's collective input and iterative process produced a solution that resonated with users, driving success and fostering a culture of trust and respect.

Collaborative decision making is a hallmark of critical thinking. By valuing diverse perspectives, addressing root causes, and embracing the iterative nature of problem solving, teams can achieve extraordinary outcomes (Lorenzo, 2017). The art of teaming transforms challenges into opportunities, demonstrating that the best decisions often emerge from collective effort and mutual respect.

- **Collaborative decision making:** Make decisions quickly by seeking input from those closest to the problem, addressing root causes, and balancing short- and long-term impacts.

- **Teaming:** Effective teamwork requires humility, curiosity, and adaptability to navigate multiple skills, cultures, and challenges in fast-paced environments.

- **Collective Creativity:** Innovation thrives on iterative processes, open debate, and integrating diverse perspectives into cohesive solutions.

Action Steps

1. How do I ensure that the voices of those closest to the problem are heard in the decision-making process?

2. Do I balance the urgency of making a decision with the need for thoughtful consideration? How?

3. How can I navigate differences in skills, cultures, or time zones within my team better?

4. How can I encourage constructive debate and discourse within my team to refine ideas?

5. Can I create an environment where opposing ideas can be integrated into innovative outcomes?

Chapter 16:

Ethical Compass—Maneuvering Moral Dilemmas

There is no need for temples; no need for complicated philosophy. Our own brain, our own heart is our temple; the philosophy is kindness. –Dalai Lama

Elliot is the well-respected head researcher at a growing pharma company. Faced with a tight deadline and increasing pressure, he decided to take a shortcut—he fudged a report to make it look like a drug was further along than it actually was. He rationalized it as a "small tweak" to buy time for the team to catch up. Nobody would notice, he thought, and the result would justify the means.

Initially, the decision seemed harmless, even beneficial. The stakeholders approved additional funding based on the optimistic report. However, soon, chinks began to appear. The team struggled to deliver, and they missed deadlines, eroding trust. When the truth emerged, the company's reputation suffered, and Elliot's credibility was irreparably damaged. A seemingly minor ethical lapse had set off a chain reaction of consequences.

What can we learn from the incident? Shortcuts in ethics rarely lead to long-term success or happiness.

Ethical Decision Making

Ethics, the cornerstone of right and wrong, is integral to every facet of life. Whether personal, social, environmental, or organizational, ethical behavior ensures that decisions are just, transparent, and sustainable. Practicing ethics—even when no one is watching—prevents harmful shortcuts and builds a foundation of trust and integrity. The ripple effect of ethical leadership can inspire teams, reinforce self-belief, and foster happiness and productivity in every area of life.

Let us look at just some benefits of being ethical:

Some of the major arguments in support of nurturing ethics are:

- **Prevention of harm:** Ethical practices avert shortcuts or actions that can damage the health and well-being of individuals and organizations.

- **Role modeling:** Ethical leadership creates a trickle-down effect, teaching teams the importance of integrity. An ethical manager inspires an ethical team.

- **Self-belief and productivity:** You can seldom lie to your own conscience and get away with it. Sticking to ethical principles reinforces belief in one's choices and, thereby, in oneself, leading to happiness and higher productivity.

- **Trust building:** there is no bigger validation than knowing you are on the right path. Ethical decision making builds trust with oneself and others, encouraging stronger relationships and greater faith in one's leadership.

Since we know how ethics can bring trust, happiness, and self-satisfaction, let us look at some ways to incorporate it into our lives.

Making Ethical Decisions

Ethical decisions are not always straightforward, but following a structured process can help ensure alignment with core values and long-term goals.

- **Define your values:** Start by identifying the core values that matter most to you, such as honesty, fairness, compassion, or responsibility. These values act as your moral compass, guiding you toward choices that reflect your principles and integrity.

- **Pause and reflect:** When faced with a dilemma, resist the urge to act impulsively. Take a moment to pause and reflect. Consider the broader implications of your decision—both immediate and long-term—and how it aligns with your values.

- **Gather Information:** Collect all relevant facts and seek diverse perspectives to gain a comprehensive understanding of the situation. Avoid making decisions based on incomplete or biased information, as this can lead to unintended consequences.

- **Evaluate options:** Thoroughly assess the available options by asking critical questions like: Who will be affected by this decision, and in what ways? Does this choice align with my core values and ethical principles? What are the potential short-term benefits and long-term risks? Weigh these factors to identify the most ethically sound option.

- **Consult trusted sources:** Discuss your dilemma with a mentor, colleague, or trusted advisor who can provide an objective perspective. Use ethical frameworks such as utilitarianism (maximizing benefits for most people) or virtue ethics (focusing on moral character) to guide your reasoning.

- **Empathize:** Put yourself in the shoes of those who will be impacted by your decision. Reflect on how you would feel if you were in their position and how your actions might influence their well-being or trust in you.

- **Choose accountability:** Be prepared to stand by your decision, taking full responsibility for its outcomes—both positive and negative. Accountability not only strengthens your credibility but also reinforces your commitment to ethical principles.

- **Practice ethical habits:** Build a habit of ethical reflection by regularly evaluating your actions and decisions. Make it a practice to learn from past dilemmas, identifying areas for growth and improvement. Over time, these habits foster consistency in making ethical choices.

- **Prioritize well-being:** Strive to find solutions that are fair and equitable, minimizing harm and maximizing well-being for all parties involved. Consider the ripple effect of your decision on individuals, teams, and the broader community.

In Practice

The next time, Elliot decides to adhere to ethical decision-making principles. He pauses and reflects on the broader consequences of his actions. He realizes the risks of misleading stakeholders by gathering information and consulting his team. Empathizing with those who will be affected by his choice—from team members to patients—he shifts his perspective. Instead of taking a shortcut, Elliot communicates transparently, gains stakeholder support for a revised timeline, and reinforces trust within his organization.

The ethical path could be more challenging in the short-term but will safeguard long-term success and trust.

Key Takeaways

- Ethical lapses, even small ones, can lead to long-term consequences for individuals and organizations.

- Define your core values and use them as a moral compass in decision making.

- Pause, gather information, and evaluate options to ensure alignment with your principles.

- Consult trusted sources and empathize with those affected by your decisions.

- Choose accountability and prioritize well-being to build trust and integrity.

- Practicing consistent ethical behavior fosters happiness, productivity, and stronger relationships.

Action Steps

1. Do I reflect daily on my decisions and whether they align with my values?

2. Have I created a list of my core ethical principles, and do I use it to review significant decisions?

3. Do I practice empathy by considering the perspectives of all stakeholders in a dilemma?

4. Do I build accountability by sharing my decisions and reasoning with a trusted mentor or peer?

5. What have I learned from past ethical dilemmas to improve my decision-making framework?

Section 4:
Application

Chapter 17:

Speak Smart—The Skill of Persuasive Communication

I define connection as the energy that exists between people when they feel seen, heard, and valued. –Brene Brown

In this section, comprising the five final chapters of this book, we shall look at ways in which all that we have talked of can be practically applied. Therefore, we shall hark back to previous case studies or scenarios and apply some of the steps involved in critical thinking and empathy-driven practical wisdom to the stories to understand how you can improve not just the way you think, act, and communicate but also carry a more positive framework of thinking and feeling in your daily life.

Let us face it, "fake it till you make it," which seems to be the governing mantra of today, can only take you so far. The purpose of this book and your life must be to improve your authentic self and make each day count in crafting the best version of yourself.

Maya's Case: Empathetic Critical Thinking in Action

We shall go back to Maya's case in Chapter 4. This was the manager, torn between the two of her most promising team members, Priya and Alec. We already saw that Maya needed to be more self-aware and exercise more empathy when dealing with the situation. A wrong accusation or even the slightest bias would only worsen the situation further. So, what did she do in future meetings between herself and the disputing employees?

- **Setting a positive tone:** Instead of sending a vague email to "settle their differences between them" as she previously did, Maya decided to hold a face-to-face meeting with Alec and Priya to address their concerns directly. She began the meeting by setting a positive intention, stating, "I want us to work together to understand each other's perspectives and find a way forward that values both of your contributions." This initial step created a collaborative and respectful tone for the discussion.

- **Employing mindful, active listening:** During the meeting, Maya applied active listening skills and set aside all other work distractions, even putting her phone on silent mode inside her desk drawer. As her team members spoke, Maya ensured her mind did not wander to the million other pressing things she had to take care of. She knew that this conversation mattered, and she anchored her attention on it. She invited Alec to speak first and share his concerns, giving him her full attention. As Alec expressed his frustration about feeling overshadowed, Maya nodded, maintained appropriate eye contact, and paraphrased his points to confirm her understanding: "Alec, it sounds like you feel your creative ideas weren't adequately recognized during the presentation. Is that correct?" Similarly, when Priya shared her perspective about her leadership efforts, Maya validated her feelings by acknowledging her hard work: "I understand you feel your guidance was critical in shaping the project's success." This approach helped both employees feel heard and respected.

- **Doing a body audit:** Maya consciously checked her posture and body language to ensure she projected calmness and openness. She sat with relaxed shoulders and uncrossed arms and maintained an open stance to signal that she was approachable and invested in resolving the conflict. Regulating her breathing, she calmed her nerves and focused her mind, allowing her to remain composed and attentive throughout the discussion. Managing her regular nervous habits, like tapping her pen or fidgeting, she maintained eye contact with whoever was speaking. Maya, thus, reinforced her role as a steady and thoughtful mediator. Soon, she saw that the more calmness she radiated, Alec and Priya also relaxed, warming to her and each other. She also paid attention to the verbal and non-verbal cues of the two in front of her to not only ensure she understood what they were saying but also to intuit what they might be feeling.

- **Balancing logic and emotions:** Maya then suggested they review the project timeline and contributions objectively.

Together, they looked at drafts, emails, and meeting notes to identify each team member's role. While this logical analysis clarified factual elements, Maya didn't overlook the emotional dynamics. She emphasized the importance of teamwork by reiterating that the project wouldn't have been as successful without the efforts of both Alec and Priya. She urged them to focus on strengthening their collaboration moving forward.

- **Listening to understand, not to respond:** Maya's ability to handle the conflict ethically and inclusively was also critical. She encouraged Alec and Priya to reflect on how their differing approaches—creativity from Alec and leadership from Priya—could complement each other in future projects. By fostering this mutual appreciation, Maya turned a divisive situation into an opportunity for growth. Additionally, she remained transparent about her decision-making process, explaining that her goal was never to assign blame but to build a stronger, more cohesive team.

- **Making emotional deposits, not withdrawals:** As the meeting concluded, Maya made emotional deposits by expressing gratitude to both Alec and Priya. She thanked them both for their honesty and for working through the situation together. She added that their willingness to address issues showed how much they cared about the team's success. This acknowledgment left both employees feeling valued and motivated to improve their collaboration.

This experience also fostered Maya's personal growth. Applying empathetic, critical thinking to address the conflict, she strengthened her leadership skills and gained greater confidence in managing team dynamics. She moved from merely understanding the issue to analyzing, evaluating, and creatively solving the problem, too. Therefore, her transition from the lower orders of Bloom's pyramid to its upper echelons is clear. Alec and Priya, in turn, learned to appreciate each other's strengths and communicate more effectively, setting a positive tone for future interactions.

Key Takeaways

- **Body audit:** Check your stance, expressions, and gestures to ensure you reflect what you would like to see mirrored in the other person. A positive, encouraging body language helps foster trust and openness.

- **Emotional deposits:** Ensure your language is attuned to the other person's sensibilities and encouraging of their efforts, and not handing out criticism.

Action Steps

1. Do I practice my body stance, gestures, expressions, and overall body language in front of a mirror, especially while rehearsing important discussions? Am I happy with what I see there?

2. Do I take adequate measures to ensure my arguments are rooted in logic, even during discussions that are personal or hold an emotional appeal for me?

3. What is one weapon I should be using more in creatively solving my problems?

Chapter 18:

Growth Mindset—Turning Setbacks into Step-Ups

Let us never negotiate out of fear. But let us never fear to negotiate. –John F. Kennedy

Negotiating is a crucial element of life. Whether it is bargaining for salary or other incentives at the workplace, getting the best deals, or just finding a more suitable way of handling problems, this is a skill that can't be ignored. Negotiation is the art of reaching an agreement without fighting and considering the perspectives of all the parties involved.

Leah's Case: Critical Thinking in Negotiating

Leah, the researcher from Chapter 3, struggled because of her impulsive personal choices, based more on assumptions and the need for exciting transformative change rather than a slow and steady approach to the choices before her. We saw how she struggled with her move to a new place, seeking "better prospects" only to be disillusioned by the loneliness, expenses, and other problems involved in being on her own.

So, what does she learn from the experience or how can she handle such a situation in the future better and negotiate a working environment more conducive to her personal and professional growth?

Objective Analysis of Information and Data

A crucial first step in Leah's decision making could be objectively analyzing the options presented to her. A promotion might offer higher pay but minimal support or mentorship, while a current role provides a solid team environment with the potential for gradual growth.

By gathering concrete data, such as the cost of living in the new city and the specific expectations of her new role, Leah can separate facts from assumptions. Instead of acting on the glamour of the promotion, she can assess the actual feasibility of managing her finances and adjusting to life in a new environment. This analytical approach grounds her decision in reliable information rather than instinct or emotion.

Anticipation of Counterarguments

Critical thinking will enable Leah to anticipate potential challenges associated with her decision. Moving to a new city means living alone, adjusting to a higher cost of living, and working without the mentorship she previously relied on. By identifying these obstacles in advance, Leah can prepare solutions.

For example, she can research networking opportunities in the new city, plan a detailed budget to manage her finances, or seek advice from colleagues who have navigated similar transitions. Anticipating these counterarguments would allow Leah to weigh the excitement of the promotion against the practical realities of her new circumstances.

Creative Problem Solving

Instead of viewing the decision as a binary choice—either accepting the promotion or staying in her current role—Leah can explore alternative solutions, too. For instance, she can negotiate with her manager for a delayed start date, giving her time to better prepare for the relocation. Alternatively, she can request remote mentorship or access to training resources to help her transition smoothly into the new role.

This creative approach will enable Leah to retain the benefits of the promotion while mitigating some of the challenges, making the decision less daunting and more balanced.

Risk Assessment

Leah's impulsive decision in the past demonstrated a lack of risk evaluation. Moving to a new city without sufficient support came with significant risks, including isolation, financial strain, and professional challenges. However, when she learns to critically assess these risks, Leah can predict potential difficulties and take steps to mitigate them.

For example, she creates a detailed budget to avoid financial miscalculations or plans for regular visits home to combat loneliness. Assessing the risks in advance will ensure that her choice aligns with her long-term goals while minimizing negative outcomes.

Adaptability

Critical thinking equips Leah with the adaptability to respond to unexpected developments dynamically. While making her decision, she keeps an open mind to new information or perspectives that influence her choice.

For instance, when she recognizes that a promotion might overwhelm her without adequate support, she revises her plan, perhaps choosing to delay the move or seek alternative growth opportunities within her current role. Adaptability allows Leah to maintain flexibility while staying focused on her objectives.

Ethical Decision Making

Finally, ethical decision making helps Leah align her choices with her core values and long-term aspirations. As a person who values collaboration and personal growth, she learns to weigh the promotion offered in terms of mentorship or teamwork. This alignment with her values provides a sense of fulfillment and confidence in her decision.

Lessons in Critical Thinking Practices

Through her experience, Leah learned the importance of applying practical critical thinking strategies in decision making. She realized that maintaining an open and positive mindset helps in reframing challenges as opportunities rather than obstacles. Active listening to other people's advice and asking clarifying questions provided her with insights she had previously overlooked. By breaking complex decisions into smaller components—such as financial feasibility, emotional impact, and career trajectory—she found it was easier to focus on specific aspects and reduce overwhelm. Comparing and evaluating information taught her how to make choices that aligned with her long-term goals.

Growth Through Reflection

Leah's decision to accept the promotion, initially driven by impulse, became a valuable learning experience. She came to understand the power of critical thinking in navigating complex choices with clarity and confidence. By reflecting on her challenges and mistakes, she gained a deeper appreciation for objective analysis, risk assessment, and adaptability. These lessons helped her move forward more deliberately and equipped her to handle future dilemmas more effectively.

Leah's journey reflects her progression through the levels of Bloom's Taxonomy, particularly as she moves from basic cognitive processes like remembering and understanding to higher-order skills such as analyzing, evaluating, and creating. Here's how her transformation aligns with Bloom's Taxonomy:

Before: Lower-Order Thinking Skills

- **Remembering:** Initially, Leah relied on instinct and surface-level information when making decisions. Her approach lacked depth, as she failed to recall or actively apply past experiences or knowledge about decision-making challenges.

- **Understanding:** Leah demonstrated limited understanding of the implications of her choices. For example, she understood the immediate appeal of the promotion (higher pay, glamour) but did not grasp the broader consequences, such as isolation, financial strain, and professional challenges.

- **Applying:** While Leah sought advice from friends, she struggled to apply their guidance in a meaningful way. Instead of evaluating their suggestions or adapting them to her situation, she acted impulsively, bypassing the critical step of applying external insights to her context.

After: HOTS

- **Analyzing:** Leah's experience taught her to break down decisions into smaller components, such as financial feasibility, emotional impact, and career growth. She learned to separate facts from assumptions and to distinguish between short-term desires and long-term goals. By analyzing the elements of a decision, she could better understand its complexities.

- **Evaluating:** Leah began to critically evaluate her options, considering risks, benefits, and alignment with her values. She learned to weigh conflicting factors, such as higher pay versus lack of mentorship, and assess how each choice would affect her long-term aspirations.

- **Creating:** Finally, Leah adopted creative problem-solving skills, allowing her to generate alternative solutions and adapt dynamically to challenges. For example, she could now negotiate for better support in a new role or explore innovative ways to achieve growth without relocating. This ability to create solutions marked her progression to the highest level of cognitive ability.

As is evident, Leah's struggles served as a catalyst for growth, propelling her into the HOTS of analyzing, evaluating, and creating. By adopting these advanced cognitive processes, Leah not only improved her decision making but also gained the ability to approach complex situations with greater clarity, confidence, and creativity.

Key Takeaways

- **Anticipating counterarguments:** This is a vital part of negotiating offers or choices in life because you get to play the devil's advocate and rally for yourself.

- **Risk-taking:** Being creative in negotiations involves taking calculated and well-timed risks based on the data and facts that you have gathered and studied.

Action Steps

1. Think of an important life choice still hanging in the balance. How would you use the steps above to negotiate the best deal for yourself?

2. What are your non-negotiables in any given situation? What would you never compromise on?

3. What are areas you would be willing to rethink if other factors were beneficial?

Chapter 19:

Beyond the Classroom—Thinking that Transforms

Economists who have studied the relationship between education and economic growth confirm what common sense suggests: The number of college degrees is not nearly as important as how well students develop cognitive skills, such as critical thinking and problem-solving ability. –Derek Bok

For a minute, let us look at Alex's case from Chapter 2 again. He was finding it extremely hard to understand why his methods of learning were failing. While he focused on memorizing facts, dates, and names, his teacher expected him to relate causes and consequences in history. In short, the teacher wanted Alex to make connections between what happened, why they happened, and possibly even comment upon how these situations could have influenced modern life or been averted.

A lot of classroom teaching still relies on drilling in facts and formulas without enough emphasis on why this information matters or how it can be used. This can create disengaged and listless learners. For instance, consider the case of a teacher who will only ask factual questions of their learners. Very soon, the learners will feel dispirited and unenthusiastic, even if they can answer all the questions. However, if a teacher makes connections between the subject and contemporary situations, news, or even popular culture, learners will understand the relevance and importance of what they are learning.

Learning is, ultimately, not about storing a lot of information in one's head. It is about challenging learners to analyze, evaluate, and create— the higher levels of Bloom's Taxonomy. If they don't develop critical thinking skills or connect knowledge to events or broader themes, learners will continue to view classroom learning as a dull list of dates and names rather than a dynamic, interconnected narrative, imparting valuable lessons about society and decision making. If a teacher fails to foster critical thinking, they not only miss an opportunity to ignite learners' curiosity but also risk alienating them from the subject altogether.

Though concrete measures for enabling critical thinking will depend on the particular subject, there are some general guidelines most teachers and learners can follow for almost all subjects. We shall look at some of these strategies in this chapter.

Critical Thinking in Classroom Teaching and Assessment

In classroom teaching and assessment, fostering critical thinking requires intentionality and structure, both in the tasks we set and the ways we evaluate learners.

Critical Thinking Assessment

Effective assessment of critical thinking begins with carefully designed tasks that can challenge learners to engage deeply with content. Bloom's Taxonomy provides a useful scaffold, emphasizing higher-order cognitive skills like analyzing, evaluating, and creating. For instance, in an English literature class, a teacher might ask learners to explore the theme of justice in *To Kill a Mockingbird* through Atticus Finch's character. Instead of summarizing the plot, learners are prompted to analyze how justice is portrayed in a racially divided society. This aligns with the higher levels of Bloom's Taxonomy, encouraging learners to evaluate and synthesize complex ideas.

The Socratic Method further supports this approach by fostering inquiry and dialogue. For example, during a debate on renewable energy, learners are guided to examine assumptions and probe deeper into questions like, "Are renewable energy sources sufficient to replace fossil fuels?" By asking follow-up questions and encouraging counterarguments, teachers stimulate critical reflection and intellectual rigor. Paul and Elder's Critical Thinking Framework (*Paul-Elder Critical Thinking Framework*, 2010), comprised of reasoning, intellectual standards, and intellectual traits, complements this method by emphasizing clarity, relevance, logic, and profundity. In a history class on World War II, teachers can ensure relevance and profundity by asking learners to connect the economic impacts of the war on women's roles in society with contemporary shifts during economic crises. This type of assessment goes beyond recall, demanding depth and breadth of understanding.

From the learner's perspective, critical thinking assessment is a twofold challenge: producing work that is clear and logical while engaging with the task's relevance. For instance, in a science lesson on ecosystems, learners might hypothesize the effects of deforestation on biodiversity. Their response must follow a logical progression, defining key terms, explaining ecological consequences, and linking them to larger environmental concerns. Clarity is equally vital; learners explaining math problems to peers must articulate their reasoning, such as, "I used the quadratic formula because the equation is not factorable." These practices ensure that their thinking is accessible and meaningful to their audience.

Theoretical Foundations

The theories underpinning critical thinking in education provide a robust foundation for these practices. Constructivist learning theory, championed by Piaget and Vygotsky (Ozer, 2004), emphasizes active knowledge construction. Vygotsky's concept of the zone of proximal development (ZPD) is particularly relevant, as it encourages tasks that are slightly beyond learners' current capabilities. For instance, a physics teacher might begin with simple projectile calculations before introducing air resistance, pushing learners to expand their understanding incrementally. Similarly, in economics, introducing a government subsidy as a variable in a supply-and-demand case study forces learners to adapt their reasoning and draw new conclusions.

Kahneman's Dual Process Theory (*Dual Process Theory*, 2019) further elucidates the cognitive processes involved in critical thinking. While intuitive, fast thinking (System 1) may dominate initial reactions, deliberate, slow thinking (System 2) is essential for thoughtful analysis. In a business class simulation, learners could evaluate two paths for a failing company: a reactive cost-cutting strategy versus an innovative long-term plan. This exercise shifts learners from reactive thinking to deliberate reasoning, requiring them to justify their decisions comprehensively.

Critical Thinking in Practice

In practice, fostering critical thinking in the classroom involves dynamic and interactive strategies. Mind mapping, for example, is a powerful tool for organizing ideas. A biology teacher might use this method to teach the human digestive system, with "digestion" as the central node and branches detailing processes like ingestion and absorption. This visual representation encourages learners to analyze relationships between concepts, enhancing their logical reasoning.

Problem-based learning offers another avenue for critical thinking. By presenting learners with real-world problems lacking definitive answers, this method fosters inquiry and collaboration. In a current events discussion, learners might research climate policies in different countries, regroup to refine their questions, and examine policy comparisons. Allowing time-sensitive research and iterative questioning mirrors the iterative nature of real-world problem solving.

Flexibility and empathy are also integral to critical thinking. Encouraging learners to take opposing perspectives broadens their understanding and challenges biases. In a debate on free speech laws, learners might argue viewpoints they personally disagree with, fostering empathy and intellectual flexibility. Similarly, a sociology class might involve writing a diary entry from the perspective of a factory worker during the Industrial Revolution, helping learners connect historical contexts to human experiences.

Assessing Critical Thinking

Assessment methods must prioritize thinking over recall, aligning with Kolb's Experiential Learning Theory (Mcleod, 2024). For example, in a STEM class, learners designing energy-efficient houses are assessed on how they conceptualize scientific principles, experiment with prototypes, and reflect on improvements. Pre-tests and post-tests in renewable energy discussions reveal how learners' understanding evolves, highlighting the value of reflection and conceptual growth.

Logicality, profundity, and clarity should remain the key criteria for assessment. Teachers must evaluate whether learners' responses are organized and evidence-based, combining unique ideas with external resources. For instance, in an art analysis of Picasso's *Guernica*, learners who connect the painting's imagery to the Spanish Civil War demonstrate deeper thinking by integrating historical research with creative interpretation.

All said and done, only through a deliberate integration of theory and practice can classrooms become vibrant spaces where critical thinking thrives.

Bonus

Here is a QR code that will take you to a reliable and validated critical thinking rubric that you can use in the assessment of your students. The rubric is shared by the author and was validated and assessed through his thesis research in 2020.

Key Takeaways

- Critical thinking in classroom teaching and assessment is a multidimensional process that requires careful planning and execution.

- Grounded in theories like Bloom's Taxonomy, the Socratic Method, and constructivist learning, effective strategies can challenge learners to analyze, evaluate, and create meaningfully.

- Practical applications such as mind mapping, problem-based learning, and empathy exercises cultivate these skills in diverse contexts.

- By assessing thinking over recall and prioritizing depth, clarity, and logic, educators not only enhance learners' intellectual abilities but also prepare them to navigate the complexities of the modern world.

Action Steps

As a teacher/learner, can I employ the following in my teaching/learning experience to enrich it?:

1. Allowing time-sensitive research: regroup and discuss, refine a research question, and create a new time limit for more research.

2. Creating two alternative paths forward: a reactive response and a critical thinking response.

3. Choosing the best path forward and justifying an answer.

4. Changing one variable and analyzing the results.

5. Taking the opposite perspective.

6. Empathizing with another perspective.

7. Creating (vs. merely giving) an output.

Chapter 20:

Be Prepared—Critical Thinking Under Pressure

Pressure is nothing more than the shadow of great opportunity. –Michael Johnson

If you remember Tara, the marketing specialist from Chapter 10, you might also remember how she succumbed to pressure and made decisions based on availability rather than the expertise of her team. If there is anything she can learn from this experience, it is that critical thinking under stress is an invaluable skill.

Stress often clouds judgment, leading to impulsive actions and suboptimal outcomes. Critical thinking techniques help mitigate this by fostering a structured, calm approach to decision making. When under stress, it is vital to pause and center yourself through mindfulness, anticipate emotional triggers, and employ logical frameworks. Challenging automatic thoughts, engaging in active problem solving, and reframing stress as a growth opportunity can transform pressure into productivity. Regular debriefs and building a support network strengthen long-term resilience.

Here's how these principles played out for Tara. You, too, can learn from her example to leverage each of the above tactics.

From Impulsivity to Strategic Action

Tara's initial approach to the high-pressure campaign revealed the pitfalls of reactive decision making. Feeling overwhelmed, she prioritized tasks based on urgency rather than importance, overlooking her team's strengths and the campaign's strategic needs. This led to inefficiency, frustration, and, ultimately, an unsatisfactory outcome. Post-campaign, Tara took a hard look at her work style and committed to applying a few practical critical thinking principles to prevent future mishaps.

Practicing Mindfulness

As we have seen, mindfulness helps you stay present and refocus, reducing the overwhelming feelings that stress can bring.

Tara began dedicating 10 minutes each morning to mindfulness exercises, focusing on her breath to ground herself. During stressful moments, she paused to take a few deep breaths, which helped her reset and approach challenges with clarity. This newfound calm enabled her to think through her decisions instead of reacting first and regretting later.

Identifying Emotional Triggers

We have already covered this in Chapter 12. Understanding what triggers your stress allows you to anticipate and prepare for emotional reactions. It will also help you reframe your emotional responses into rational responses.

Reflecting on the campaign, Tara realized that her anxiety about meeting the client's high expectations had pushed her to micromanage. She identified her tendency to panic under tight deadlines, which often led her to act hastily. In recognizing this trigger, Tara prepared herself to stay composed and methodical in future projects. Every time she panicked, she knew she had to step back. She would only look at the issue once the immediate fear had passed and she had a grip over herself.

Using Decision-Making Frameworks

A structured approach ensures logical thinking even in high-pressure moments. Weighing the pros and cons or doing a Strengths, Weaknesses, Opportunities, and Threats (SWOT) analysis can really be a game-changer.

For her next campaign, Tara employed a SWOT analysis to evaluate her team's capabilities and the client's needs. This structured approach guided her in delegating tasks based on the strengths of the team that could be converted into opportunities. She also prioritized tasks strategically, ensuring that critical milestones were addressed first. She proactively thought about the pitfalls that could arise in the process and put in place some remedial interventions that might work. This converted the potential weaknesses and threats into navigable points.

Challenging Automatic Thoughts

Stress often triggers unhelpful cognitive distortions like catastrophizing or black-and-white thinking. This will only make solving problems even tougher. A set of rational go-to questions can always make this easier.

Tara worked to counter cognitive distortions by asking herself rational questions. When she felt overwhelmed, she reframed her thoughts: "What evidence suggests my team is incapable?" or "What can I adjust to ensure success?" This practice helped her see the campaign as a solvable challenge rather than an insurmountable problem. This also made her general outlook more positive.

Engaging in Stress Simulations

Practicing under controlled stress conditions helps build mental endurance. Just as simulated driving experience can contribute to your skill as a driver, foreseeing problems and tackling them can also be helpful.

To improve her tolerance for pressure, Tara began role-playing stressful scenarios with her mentor, simulating high-pressure meetings or team miscommunications. Her mentor threw various situations at Tara, slowly increasing in complexity, which she would try to solve in a certain agreed timeframe. Such exercises strengthened her mental endurance and her ability to think critically under stress. She noticed that the more she practiced, the better she got at these challenges. She could tackle them faster and with less hesitation and self-doubt. This also translated into her handling real-life problems at work better.

Apart from the above, building mental habits of logic and analysis can also improve critical thinking over time. Some other ways of boosting your logical abilities could include things like:

- playing strategy games like chess or sudoku.

- reading articles and identifying biases or assumptions.

- practicing asking "why" questions more often to deepen your understanding.

Practicing Active Problem Solving

Instead of looking at the problem, focusing on solutions keeps your mind grounded and engaged. During the next campaign, Tara broke down the project into smaller, actionable steps. She tackled one priority at a time, ensuring clear communication with her team. This method prevented duplication of effort and minimized miscommunications overall.

Cultivating Emotional Regulation

Managing your emotions helps you think more clearly. How you do this can be wholly up to you. The key is merely to channel your emotions positively.

Journaling became Tara's outlet for processing her emotions. Writing about her fears and frustrations allowed her to release pent-up tension and approach her work more rationally. Additionally, she committed to regular exercise, which boosted her overall mental and physical resilience.

Reframing Stress as a Challenge

When you view stress as an opportunity, it activates problem solving rather than avoidance. Tara shifted her mindset from dreading high-pressure campaigns to seeing them as opportunities to grow further. She often reminded herself that every challenge was a chance to refine her leadership skills and deliver exceptional results. Constantly reinforcing such ideas helped her see her role and choices better.

Debriefing and Building a Support System

However good or bad the outcomes are, reflecting on how you handled stress in a situation helps reinforce effective habits. Trusted friends, mentors, or colleagues can often offer insights and objectivity when you're struggling to think critically. Therefore, regular check-in meetings to share and discuss challenges with your support network build a habit of collaborative problem solving.

After another campaign, which was more successful than any of her earlier ones, even as Tara enjoyed the sweet taste of success, she did not neglect the debrief with her team. Together, they celebrated wins and discussed areas for further improvement. She leaned on her mentor and colleagues during the process for feedback and perspective, recognizing the value of collaborative problem solving.

Key Takeaways

- **Critical thinking under stress**: Stress often clouds judgment, but critical thinking techniques like mindfulness, logical frameworks, and reframing stress as an opportunity can transform pressure into productivity.

- **Mindfulness as a tool**: Regular mindfulness practices help ground oneself during stressful moments, enabling better clarity and decision making.

- **Structured decision making**: Using tools like SWOT analysis ensures logical and strategic delegation of tasks, minimizing inefficiencies.

- **Simulated stress scenarios**: Practicing high-pressure scenarios in controlled settings strengthens mental endurance and critical thinking skills.

- **Reframing stress positively**: Viewing stress as a growth opportunity fosters a proactive mindset and leadership development.

- **Debriefing and collaboration**: Reflecting on outcomes and engaging with a support system reinforces effective habits and encourages collaborative problem solving.

Action Steps

1. How do I typically react under stress? Can I identify instances where stress affected the quality of my decisions?

2. How might dedicating 10 minutes a day to mindfulness impact my ability to handle stress?

3. What structured critical thinking approach can I apply to tackle a current challenge?

4. How might shifting my mindset about challenges impact my growth and success?

5. Who in my support system can offer objective feedback or collaborative problem solving when I'm under stress?

Chapter 21:

Think Again—The Habit of Lifelong Inquiry

It is better to debate a question without settling it than to settle a question without debating it. –Joseph Joubert

What this book has been driving at is that critical thinking is an essential skill for daily life, offering a range of benefits. By analyzing your options thoroughly, you can identify potential pitfalls and make informed choices, avoiding unnecessary stress and loss. It streamlines processes, bypassing trial-and-error approaches, and fosters creative yet logical problem solving. Critical thinking encourages self-reflection, helping you recognize biases and make mindful decisions aligned with your values. It enhances communication, empathy, and conflict resolution by promoting an understanding of others' perspectives. This skill sharpens curiosity, fuels continuous learning, builds confidence, and enables sound, pressure-tested decisions that balance practicality with moral and societal considerations, empowering independence and resilience.

Thinking critically doesn't have to be for the "big," work-related, earth-shattering decisions alone in life. It can be for the every day, small, mundane choices you need to make daily. In this last chapter, we shall look at some extremely common, perhaps even boring, daily experiences and how they can be handled better by practicing critical thinking. We shall look forward to making critical thinking second nature to your existence.

Critical Thinking in Daily Life: A Guide to Empowerment

Critical thinking is not reserved for scholars, analysts, or professionals in high-stakes industries. It is an everyday tool that can transform the way you navigate the complexities of life. Let us see how easy it can be to apply this tool.

Evaluating News or Social Media Posts

In a world saturated with information, critical thinking is your safeguard against misinformation. Imagine you stumble upon a sensational headline online. Instead of hitting the share button impulsively, you pause to evaluate the content. Who wrote this article? What evidence supports the claims made? Is the tone or framing biased? By checking the source, reading the article fully, and cross-referencing it with reputable outlets, you ensure the accuracy of the information you consume and share.

Questions to ask:

- Who wrote this?

- What evidence supports this claim?

- Is this biased?

Making Health Decisions

Health trends may come and go, but your well-being depends on discernment. Let's say a friend recommends a trendy new diet. Instead of diving in headfirst, you research its benefits and risks, ensuring it aligns with your health goals. Consulting a healthcare professional further validates your decision. Thinking critically, you can avoid blindly following fads and prioritize what's truly beneficial for you.

Questions to ask:

- What are the potential risks?

- What scientific evidence supports this theory?

Budgeting and Spending

Your financial decisions shape your lifestyle and future. Imagine you're tempted to purchase the latest gadget. Before swiping your card, you compare prices, read reviews, and assess whether the item is a necessity or a passing desire. Critical thinking ensures that your spending aligns with your priorities and long-term goals.

Questions to ask:

- Will this product truly add value to my life?
- Is this the best time to buy?

Resolving Conflicts

Conflicts are inevitable, but how you handle them can make all the difference. Suppose a colleague blames you for a mistake at work. Instead of reacting defensively, you gather facts, listen to their perspective, and calmly discuss the issue. In this manner, you can identify constructive solutions that preserve relationships and foster mutual respect.

Questions to Ask Yourself:

- What proof supports their claim?
- How can I address this constructively?

Planning Your Day

Time management is a critical skill, and critical thinking enhances it. With a long to-do list ahead, you might feel overwhelmed. Instead of tackling tasks randomly, you evaluate their urgency and importance. By prioritizing effectively, you ensure that essential goals are met without compromising on quality.

Questions to ask:

- What tasks align with my goals?
- What can be delegated or postponed?

Assessing Relationships

Healthy relationships require understanding and reflection. Imagine a friend frequently cancels plans at the last minute. Instead of assuming they're indifferent, you consider their circumstances and communicate your feelings. Critical thinking helps you navigate relationships with empathy and clarity.

Questions to Ask Yourself:

- Is there a pattern or reason behind this behavior?

- How can I express my concerns effectively without alienating them?

Choosing Entertainment

Even leisure can benefit from critical thinking. When selecting a movie to watch with friends who have different preferences, you weigh everyone's tastes. By suggesting a genre that balances interests, you ensure an enjoyable experience for all.

Questions to Ask Yourself:

- What options cater to the majority's interests?

- How can I compromise while still enjoying myself?

Cooking or Meal Planning

Flexibility in the kitchen is a hallmark of critical thinking. Suppose a recipe calls for an ingredient you don't have. Rather than abandoning the dish, you research suitable substitutes or adapt the recipe to what's available. This resourcefulness minimizes waste and sparks creativity.

Questions to ask:

- What alternatives will achieve the same result?

- How can I avoid wasting ingredients?

Helping Children With Homework

Guiding children's learning fosters critical thinking in you and them. When your child struggles with a math problem, resist the urge to solve it for them. Instead, guide them through the process, encouraging them to think critically and find the solution independently.

Questions to ask:

- What steps can help them understand?
- How can I simplify the explanation?

Evaluating Career or Life Choices

Life's big decisions demand thoughtful consideration. Whether you're contemplating a career change or moving to a new city, critical thinking helps you weigh the pros and cons, research the implications, and align your choices with long-term goals. This deliberate approach ensures your decisions are both practical and meaningful.

Questions to ask:

- Does this shift align with my goals?
- What challenges might I face?

Critical thinking is more than a skill; it's a mindset that empowers you to face life's complexities with confidence and clarity. The right questions at the right time, coupled with an attitude of curiosity and logic in any given situation, make you better equipped to make informed decisions, solve problems, and build meaningful relationships.

Remember, each day presents opportunities to practice critical thinking —embrace them and watch your life joyfully and meaningfully unfold.

Key Takeaways

- **Critical Thinking is an everyday tool**: It's not just for scholars or professionals but can transform daily life decisions, from evaluating news to managing relationships.

- **Evaluating information**: Critical thinking safeguards against misinformation by encouraging scrutiny of sources, evidence, and biases before acting or sharing.

- **Informed health decisions**: Avoid blindly following trends by researching risks, benefits, and consulting experts to make choices aligned with personal health goals.

- **Financial prudence**: Applying critical thinking to budgeting and spending ensures alignment with long-term priorities rather than impulsive desires.

- **Conflict resolution**: Handling conflicts constructively involves gathering facts, listening actively, and seeking mutually respectful solutions.

- **Time management**: Prioritizing tasks based on urgency and importance prevents overwhelm and ensures quality results.

- **Relationship assessment**: Understanding patterns and communicating effectively fosters healthier, more empathetic relationships.

- **Creative problem solving**: From cooking with substitutes to helping children with homework, critical thinking sparks resourcefulness and fosters learning.

- **Entertainment choices**: Balancing different preferences ensures enjoyable experiences for all while practicing compromise and inclusivity.

- **Major life choices**: Critical thinking helps navigate significant decisions, ensuring they are practical, meaningful, and aligned with long-term goals.

1. How can I ensure that I don't contribute to consuming or spreading misinformation?

2. How can I balance health trends with evidence-based choices?

3. What strategies can I adopt to manage my time more effectively?

4. How often do I consider others' preferences when planning leisure activities?

5. How can I cultivate a mindset of curiosity and logic to face life's complexities with confidence?

Conclusion:

The World Needs Thinkers

Going back to the Chilean mining accident, the episode teaches us the importance of not just critical thinking but collaborative, creative, and empathetic thinking to save lives. It serves as the best illustration of everything this book has been trying to capture because it enshrines the following principles we have discussed at length:

- remaining calm under intense pressure to perform

- not being too quick to react but productively procrastinating enough to find the best solution possible

- breaking down a huge problem into manageable chunks of action

- finding the courage to ask for and receive help when necessary

- remembering that our choices have a ripple effect on many lives around us

As you close this book, take a moment to reflect on the journey you've undertaken. Each chapter has been a step toward mastering the art of critical thinking —a skill that will serve as your compass in life's challenges, opportunities, and uncertainties.

Critical thinking is not just a tool for solving problems or making decisions; it is a way of life. It empowers you to question assumptions, break free from biases, and see the world through a lens of curiosity and possibility. It encourages resilience in the face of setbacks and cultivates a positive mindset that transforms obstacles into stepping stones.

But this is just the beginning. The principles and techniques outlined here are not a one-time exercise; they are habits to be practiced and refined daily. Like a muscle, your ability to think critically grows stronger with consistent use. When faced with a dilemma, remember the frameworks and strategies you've learned—pause, reflect, and approach the situation with renewed focus and confidence.

You now possess the tools to disaggregate complexities into manageable parts, synthesize diverse perspectives, and make thoughtful, informed decisions. These skills will not only enhance your personal and professional life but will also contribute to a more thoughtful and empathetic world.

Remember, growth need not necessarily be linear. There will be moments of doubt or frustration, but these are merely opportunities to deepen your understanding and sharpen your thinking. So, embrace them with an open mind and a willingness to learn.

Your journey with critical thinking doesn't end here; it evolves with you. Seek out challenges that stretch your cognitive boundaries. Engage in meaningful conversations. Question the status quo. Most importantly, remain committed to the practice of self-reflection and continuous learning.

The world needs thinkers—individuals who can rise above the noise, who value integrity and truth, and who are unafraid to hope. You are now equipped to be one of them. May your decisions reflect not just what is logical but also what is compassionate and inspired by a vision of a better future.

Go forth with confidence, curiosity, and the unwavering belief that you are capable of achieving great things. The next steps are yours to take! All the best! If you liked the book, please feel free to leave a review on Amazon or press the star rating at the end of this book.

About the Author

Eric J. Kelly stepped into the specialization of positive critical thinking 15 years ago. Working in the education sector, he introduced the growth of higher-order thinking skills (HOTS) at all its levels—elementary school, junior high school, high school, and university, and extended his insights into corporate training for both national and international companies.

He completed a master's degree, including a thesis in critical thinking, in 2022. The valid and reliable study included teaching techniques and measurement tools used by Eric, which consistently showed that HOTS can improve drastically in weeks, not years, especially when employing deliberate thinking practice.

His work has only proven what he has known all along—that thinking growth can create confident, resilient, and creative individuals who relish the challenges that life throws their way.

Eric's other work includes *Critical Thinking for Teens - The Art of Problem Solving: The Thinking Mind Process for Logical Decision Making with a Cognitive Confidence and Resilient Mindset* (2025), which you can access by scanning the following QR code:

References

Ackerman, C. (2018, July 25). *What is neuroplasticity? A psychologist explains.* Positive Psychology. https://positivepsychology.com/neuroplasticity/

Angela Davis. (2010, March 1). National Museum of African American History and Culture. https://nmaahc.si.edu/angela-davis

Aviv, R. (2017, July 18). *The philosopher of feelings.* The New Yorker. https://www.newyorker.com/magazine/2016/07/25/martha-nussbaums-moral-philosophies

Balino, M. (2023, October 11). *Kendall's and Marzano's New Taxonomy ppt.* SlideShare. https://www.slideshare.net/slideshow/kendalls-and-marzanos-new-taxonomy-ppt/262051421#4

Beckman, T. (2020, October 29). *What is active recall? How to use it to ace your exams.* Brainscape Academy. https://www.brainscape.com/academy/active-recall-definition-studying/

Bernard Shaw, G. (n.d.) *George Bernard Shaw quotes. "The possibilities are numerous once we decide to act and not react."* (n.d.). Quotefancy. https://quotefancy.com/quote/811984/George-Bernard-Shaw-The-possibilities-are-numerous-once-we-decide-to-act-and-not-react

The best design thinking exercises for each phase of a project. (2022, September 15). Voltage Control. https://voltagecontrol.com/blog/the-best-design-thinking-exercises-for-each-phase-of-a-project/

Bloom's revised taxonomy. (2019). Colorado College. https://www.coloradocollege.edu/other/assessment/how-to-assess-learning/learning-outcomes/blooms-revised-taxonomy.html

Bloom's taxonomy of cognitive levels (revised). (n.d.). North Carolina State University.

https://faculty.chass.ncsu.edu/slatta/hi216/learning/bloom.ht
m

Bok, D. (n.d.). *Derek Bok quotes*. Quotefancy.
https://quotefancy.com/quote/1098725/Derek-Bok-
Economists-who-have-studied-the-relationship-between-
education-and-economic

Boorstin, D. J. (n.d.). *Daniel J. Boorstin quotes*. Goodreads.
https://www.goodreads.com/quotes/68927-the-greatest-
enemy-of-knowledge-is-not-ignorance-it-is

Bossidy, L. (2024). *Lawrence Bossidy quotes*. A-Z Quotes.
https://www.azquotes.com/quotes/topics/systematic.html

Brown, B. (n.d.). *Brené Brown quotes*. Goodreads.
https://www.goodreads.com/quotes/417390-i-define-
connection-as-the-energy-that-exists-between-people

Buckle, H. T. (n.d.). *Henry Thomas Buckle quotes*. Goodreads.
https://www.goodreads.com/author/quotes/999423.Henry_T
homas_Buckle

Chang, R. (2014). *How to make hard choices*. Ted.com; TED Talks.
https://www.ted.com/talks/ruth_chang_how_to_make_hard_
choices

Changwong, K., Sukkamart, A., & Sisan, B. (2018). Enhancing Thai high
school student critical thinking capability: A new learning
management model. *Asia-Pacific Social Science Review, 18*(1).
https://doi.org/10.59588/2350-8329.1157

Cherry, K. (2024, February 22). *13 types of common cognitive biases that might
be impairing your judgment*. Verywell Mind.
https://www.verywellmind.com/cognitive-biases-distort-
thinking-2794763#toc-other-kinds-of-cognitive-bias

Cherry, K. (2024 a, May 7). *How cognitive biases influence how you think and
act*. Verywell Mind. https://www.verywellmind.com/what-is-a-
cognitive-bias-2794963#toc-types-of-cognitive-bias

Cooks-Campbell, A. (2023, November 28). *Emotional triggers: What they are and 9 tips deal with them.* Better Up. https://www.betterup.com/blog/triggers#what-are-triggers?

Critical thinking in everyday life: 9 strategies. (2017). The Foundation for Critical Thinking. https://www.criticalthinking.org/pages/critical-thinking-in-everyday-life-9-strategies/512

Dalai Lama. (2010). *Dalai Lama quotes.* Goodreads. https://www.goodreads.com/quotes/tag/ethics

Davina. (2020, July 3). *The value of thinking top-down versus bottom-up.* Clarity First. https://clarityfirstprogram.com/the-value-of-thinking-top-down-versus-only-thinking-bottom-up/

DeMers, J. (2015, July). *How to change your mindset to see problems as opportunities.* IInc. https://www.inc.com/jayson-demers/how-to-change-your-mindset-to-see-problems-as-opportunities.html

Difference between Bottom-up model and top-down model. (2019, October 21). GeeksforGeeks. https://www.geeksforgeeks.org/difference-between-bottom-up-model-and-top-down-model/

DiLeo, M. (2024, February 7). *5W2H problem-solving method.* Management and Strategy Institute. https://www.msicertified.com/blog/5w2h-training/

Dual process theory: A simple summary. (2019, July 11). The World of Work Project. https://worldofwork.io/2019/07/dual-process-theory/

The Editors of Encyclopedia Britannica. (2025, January 4). *Stephen Hawking. Encyclopedia Britannica.* Retrieved on January 10, 2025. https://www.britannica.com/biography/Stephen-Hawking

Edmondson, A. (2018). How to turn a group of strangers into a team [Video]. *TED.* https://www.ted.com/talks/amy_edmondson_how_to_turn_a_group_of_strangers_into_a_team?subtitle=en

8 powerful design thinking exercises for your next workshop. (2023, April 25). SEI | Business & Technology Management Consulting Firm. https://www.sei.com/insights/article/8-powerful-design-thinking-exercises-for-your-next-workshop/

8-step problem-solving process. (n.d.). University Human Resources - the University of Iowa. https://hr.uiowa.edu/development/organizational-development/process-change/8-step-problem-solving-process

Evaluating online information: Logical fallacies in social media. (2024, July 26). Iowa University Libraries. https://guides.lib.uiowa.edu/c.php?g=849536&p=6077643

Facione, P. A. (1990). *Executive summary: Delphi Project: Critical thinking-A statement of expert consensus for purposes of educational assessment and instruction* (pp. 1–21). Insight Assessment. https://www.researchgate.net/publication/242279575_Critical _Thinking_A_Statement_of_Expert_Consensus_for_Purposes _of_Educational_Assessment_and_Instruction

Fact-checking the news. (n.d.). Australian National University Library. https://libguides.anu.edu.au/c.php?g=942795&p=6875771

Frank, T. (2020, July 17). *How to remember more of what you learn with spaced repetition.* College Info Geek. https://collegeinfogeek.com/spaced-repetition-memory-technique/

Gleeson, J. (2021, September 7). *Judith Butler: "We need to rethink the category of woman."* The Guardian. https://www.theguardian.com/lifeandstyle/2021/sep/07/judith-butler-interview-gender

Grant, A. M. (2017). *Originals: how non-conformists change the world.* Wh Allen. (Original work published 2016)

Hancock, J. (2024). *Six Thinking Hats.* Mindtools. https://www.mindtools.com/ajlpp1e/six-thinking-hats

Henriksen, D., Richardson, C., & Shack, K. (2020). Mindfulness and creativity: Implications for thinking and learning. *Thinking skills and* *creativity*, *37*, 100689. https://doi.org/10.1016/j.tsc.2020.100689

Hill, L. (2015). How to manage for collective creativity [Video]. *Ted.* https://www.ted.com/talks/linda_hill_how_to_manage_for_c ollective_creativity?subtitle=en

Hillier, W. (2021, July 15). *What is a decision tree and how is it used?* CareerFoundry. https://careerfoundry.com/en/blog/data-analytics/what-is-a-decision-tree/

Howes, L. (2018, July 9). *Dr. Jordan Peterson on responsibility and meaning.* Lewis Howes. https://lewishowes.com/podcast/jordan-peterson-on-responsibility-and-meaning/

H.R.6971 - 117th Congress (2021-2022): Educating Against Misinformation and Disinformation Act. (2021). Congress.gov. https://www.congress.gov/bill/117th-congress/house-bill/6971

Infante, H., & Government of Chile. (2010). First test descent [Online image]. In *Wikimedia Commons.* https://commons.wikimedia.org/wiki/File:First_test_descent_ %285077055298%29.jpg

Jeffrey P. Bezos. (2025, January 17). Academy of Achievement. https://achievement.org/achiever/jeffrey-p-bezos/

Johnson, M., & Dunnell, T. (2023, May 9). *20 quotes about dealing with pressure.* Inspiring Quotes. https://www.inspiringquotes.com/20-quotes-about-dealing-with-pressure/ZFpIfZW3LQAHBO88

Joubert, J. (n.d.). *Joseph Joubert quotes.* Goodreads. https://www.goodreads.com/quotes/227289-it-is-better-to-debate-a-question-without-settling-it

Kahneman, D. (2024). *Top 13 heuristics quotes.* A-Z Quotes. https://www.azquotes.com/quotes/topics/heuristics.html

Kennedy, J. F., & Overvest, M. (2021, December 2). *Negotiation quotes – 25 legendary quotes full of wisdom*. Procurement Tactics. https://procurementtactics.com/negotiation-quotes/

Laranjeira, C., & Querido, A. (2022). Hope and Optimism as an Opportunity to Improve the "Positive Mental Health" Demand. *Frontiers in Psychology, 13*, 827320. https://doi.org/10.3389/fpsyg.2022.827320

Leadbeater, C. W. (n.d.). *Charles W. Leadbeater quotes*. Goodreads. https://www.goodreads.com/quotes/359757-you-are-what-you-share

Le Guin, U. K. (n.d.). *Ursula K. Le Guin quotes*. Goodreads. https://www.goodreads.com/quotes/9530891-there-are-no-right-answers-to-wrong-questions

Levy, S. (2025, January 15). *Steve Jobs. Encyclopedia Britannica*. Retrieved on January 16, 2025. https://www.britannica.com/money/Steve-Jobs

List of cognitive biases and heuristics. (2023). The Decision Lab. https://thedecisionlab.com/biases

Lorenzo, R. (2017, October 25). *How diversity makes teams more innovative*. TED. https://www.ted.com/talks/rocio_lorenzo_how_diversity_makes_teams_more_innovative?subtitle=en

MacLaine, S. (2024). *50 negativity quotes to help keep your job search positive*. Indeed Career Guide. https://ca.indeed.com/career-advice/career-development/negativity-quotes

Magee, J. F. (1964). *Decision trees for decision making*. Harvard Business Review. https://hbr.org/1964/07/decision-trees-for-decision-making

Marie Curie the scientist. (2015). Marie Curie. https://www.mariecurie.org.uk/about-us/our-history/marie-curie-the-scientist

Marks, G. (2024, November 27). *Why Google's Notebook LM is a killer app for small business.* Medium. https://genemarks.medium.com/why-googles-notebooklm-is-a-killer-app-for-small-business-72e5e6ce8cce

Marzano, R. J., & Kendall, J. S. (2007). *The new taxonomy of educational objectives.* Corwin Press. https://www.ifeet.org/files/The-New-taxonomy-of-Educational-Objectives.pdf

Mason, C. (2021, November 9). *Iris Murdoch: what the writer and philosopher can teach us about friendship.* The Conversation. https://theconversation.com/iris-murdoch-what-the-writer-and-philosopher-can-teach-us-about-friendship-167819

McHugh, C., & TEDx Talks. (2013). The art of being yourself [Video]. *YouTube.* https://www.youtube.com/watch?v=veEQQ-N9xWU

McIvor, M. (2021, August 2). *The logic tree: The ultimate critical thinking framework.* Globis Insights. https://globisinsights.com/career-skills/critical-thinking/logic-tree/

Mcleod, S. (2024, February 2). *Kolb's Learning Styles and Experiential Learning Cycle.* Simply Psychology. https://www.simplypsychology.org/learning-kolb.html

Mind mapping writing centre learning guide: How do I get started with mind mapping?. (2014). *The University of Adelaide.* https://www.adelaide.edu.au/writingcentre/sites/default/files/docs/learningguide-mindmapping.pdf

Outlaw, F. (2013, January 10). *Watch your thoughts, they become words; watch your words, they become actions.* Quoteinvestigator. https://quoteinvestigator.com/2013/01/10/watch-your-thoughts/

Ozer, O. (2004, October 1). *Constructivism in Piaget and Vygotsky.* The Fountain Magazine. https://fountainmagazine.com/all-issues/2004/issue-48-october-december-2004/constructivism-in-piaget-and-vygotsky

Pallardy, R. (2024, October 16). *Chile mine rescue of 2010. Encyclopedia Britannica.* Retrieved on January 9, 2025. https://www.britannica.com/event/Chile-mine-rescue-of-2010

Paul-Elder critical thinking framework: Ideas to action. (2010). University of Louisville. https://louisville.edu/ideastoaction/about/criticalthinking/fra mework

Paul, R. (n.d.). *Richard Paul quotes.* Goodreads. https://www.goodreads.com/author/quotes/223972.Richard_ Paul

Pre-Work | Problem solving 101 root cause analysis & logic trees. (n.d.). https://projects.iq.harvard.edu/files/sila/files/fullerton_proble m_solving_101_pre_reading.pdf

Rich, A. (n.d.). *Top 25 critical thinking quotes.* A-Z Quotes. https://www.azquotes.com/quotes/topics/critical-thinking.html

Schwartz, B., & TED. (2009). Our loss of wisdom [Video]. *YouTube.* https://www.youtube.com/watch?v=1A-zdh_bQBo

SCQA: Situation, complication, question, and answer. (n.d.). Corporate Finance Institute. https://corporatefinanceinstitute.com/resources/career/scqa/

7 practical ways to apply active recall when studying. (2022, August 1). Goodnotes. https://www.goodnotes.com/blog/active-recall-studying

Simon Sinek at Amsterdam Business Forum 2025. (2025). Denk Producties. https://www.denkproducties.nl/experts/simon-sinek-en

Škobalj, E. (2018). Mindfulness and critical thinking: Why should mindfulness be the foundation of the educational process? *Universal Journal of Educational Research, 6*(6), 1365–1372. https://doi.org/10.13189/ujer.2018.060628

Susanne K. Langer. (n.d.). Internet Encyclopedia of Philosophy. https://iep.utm.edu/langer/

Top-down approach vs. bottom-up approach. (2013, September 15). Simplilearn. https://www.simplilearn.com/top-down-approach-vs-bottom-up-approach-article

Watch your thoughts, they become words; watch your words, they become actions. (2013, January 10). Quote Investigator. https://quoteinvestigator.com/2013/01/10/watch-your-thoughts/

Werner, J. (2024, December 17). New functionality from Google Notebook LM is pretty amazing. *Forbes.* https://www.forbes.com/sites/johnwerner/2024/12/17/new-functionality-from-google-notebook-lm-is-pretty-amazing/

What is a 5W2H analysis? (And how to use one effectively). (2022, June 25). Indeed Career Guide. https://www.indeed.com/career-advice/career-development/5w2h-analysis

What is brainstorming? 10 effective techniques you can use. (2016, June 5). The Interaction Design Foundation. https://www.interaction-design.org/literature/topics/brainstorming?srsltid=AfmBOoo UJRWvDcFlEqBP5O5eRK3G1mxYhzrDF8AnFr1nzfkO-4Pv-vBF

What is problem-solving? Steps, process & techniques. (2024). Asq.org. https://asq.org/quality-resources/problem-solving?srsltid=AfmBOoq-o5Jk0r8FpndEWga57Mn5TJZCOhTbGzz3xhVogxMeJ7RuQE gD